THE CISTERCIAN FATHERS SERIES: NUMBER THIRTY-FIVE

GERTRUD THE GREAT OF HELFTA

THE HERALD OF GOD'S LOVING-KINDNESS:
BOOKS ONE AND TWO

Translated, with an introduction and notes, by
Alexandra Barratt

Cistercian Publications
Kalamazoo, Michigan

Gertrud(e) the Great, 1256–1302

This translation is based on the critical edition of Pierre Doyère,
Gertrude d'Helfta: Œuvres spiritualles II: Le Héraut (Livres I et II).
Paris: Editions du Cerf, 1968.

The work of Cistercian Publications is made possible in part
by support from Western Michigan University to
The Institute of Cistercian Studies

Library of Congress Cataloguing-in-Publication Data

Gertrud, the Great, Saint, 1256–1302.
  [Legatus divinae pietatis. English]
  The herald of God's loving kindness / Gertrud the Great of
Helfta : translated and annotated by Alexandra Barratt.
    p. cm. — (The Cistercian Fathers series : no. 35)
  Translation of: Legatus divinae pietatis.
  Includes bibliographical references.
  ISBN 0-87907-055-2 (alk. paper). — ISBN 0-87907-455-8
(pbk. : alk. paper)
  1. Gertrude, the Great, Saint, 1256–1302. 2. Christian saints
—Germany—Biography. 3. Mystics—Germany—Biography.
I. Barratt, Alexandra. II. Title. III. Series.
BX4700.G6A3   1991
248.2'2'092—dc20
[B]   91-18531
                                           CIP

Printed in the United States of America

THE CISTERCIAN FATHERS SERIES: NUMBER THIRTY-FIVE

Gertrud the Great of Helfta

THE HERALD OF GOD'S LOVING-KINDNESS:
BOOKS ONE AND TWO

TABLE OF CONTENTS

INTRODUCTION

THOUGH IT APPEARS IN THE CISTERCIAN FATHERS Series, this volume contains the writings of two women who were probably cistercian, but possibly benedictine, nuns: Saint Gertrud the Great (1256–1302), and her biographer, both from the monastery of Helfta, near modern Eisleben in eastern Germany. Their writings, despite Gertrud's acknowledged place in the history of spirituality, have never enjoyed wide circulation in English translation, and it is to be hoped that the nuns of Helfta may now at last obtain a timely hearing among an English-speaking audience.

HELFTA

Was Helfta a benedictine or cistercian foundation? A group of 'grey sisters' from Halberstadt—nuns who had adopted the cistercian habit of unbleached wool—founded the monastery at Helfta in 1258, which would apparently make it part of the cistercian movement. But Helfta was never under the jurisdiction of Cîteaux and was in any case founded after 1228, the year in which the cistercian general chapter forbade the establishment of any more foundations for women and put an end to cistercian involvement in the spiritual direction of women under vows. Helfta's customs however seem to have been those of Cîteaux and certainly the works of Cîteaux's most famous son, Saint Bernard, were extremely influential there.

Helfta's external history was troubled. Pillaged in 1285, placed under interdict in or around 1295, destroyed in 1342, reestablished in 1346, it was finally dissolved two hundred years later. But it has passed into history for its brief but' spectacular flowering in the latter half of the thirteenth century as a centre of mystical and intellectual activity.[1]

THE HISTORICAL BACKGROUND

Helfta's tribulations during the thirteenth century are a reflection of the situation of the time, a period of uncertainty, unrest and disorder in Germany. The Hohenstaufen Holy Roman emperor, Frederick II (1197–1250), brought up in Sicily, had taken little interest in the northern part of his empire. He disliked its 'long winters, muddy towns, dark forests and rugged castles'.[2] Preoccupied with affairs in Italy, he pursued a policy of appeasement toward the German princes, both lay and ecclesiastical, who were theoretically imperial vassals. The Pragmatic Sanctions, or statutes, of 1220 and 1232 granted them various privileges: control over currency, taxation and judicial matters. Moreover Frederick supported these increasingly independent feudal lords against the towns of Germany, a policy which was responsible for the revolt of his own son Henry in 1234. The revolt was put down, Henry died in captivity, and Frederick placed a more pliable offspring, Conrad, in charge of Germany. But this did not bring peace. In 1245 Pope Innocent III 'deposed' Frederick himself, who had long been under excommunication, and until his death in Apulia in 1250 the emperor was preoccupied with a series of papally-inspired revolts.

---

[1]On Helfta, see Pierre Doyère, ed., *Gertrude d'Helfta: Oeuvres Spirituelles* (Paris, 1968) II: 9–13; Pierre Debognie, 'Commencement et recommencements de la dévotion au coeur de Jésus', *Le Coeur* (Paris: Études Carmélitaines: 1950) 163; Sister Mary Jeremy [Finnegan OP], '*Similitudines* in the Writing of Saint Gertrude of Helfta', *Medieval Studies* 19 (1957) 48–9; L. Eckenstein, *Women Under Monasticism* (Cambridge, 1896) 328–53; Caroline Walker Bynum, *Jesus As Mother* (Berkeley and Los Angeles, 1982) 170–262; Elizabeth A. Petroff, ed., *Medieval Women's Visionary Literature* (New York and Oxford, 1986) 207–230.

[2]Geoffrey Barraclough, *Origins of Modern Germany* (Oxford, 1947) 220.

Between 1250 and 1273 Germany had, in effect, no ruler. During this 'terrible time without an emperor', the Great Interregnum, there was a plethora of *reges Romanorum*, as those emperors who had not yet been crowned in Rome were known. Frederick's son Conrad IV, who died in 1254, left a two year-old son, Conradin. This 'last of the Hohenstaufens' imprudently ventured into Italy, only to be captured and publicly executed while still in his teens. 1257, the year which marked the nadir of imperial prestige, saw the elections of two emperors: Richard of Cornwall, younger brother of Henry III of England, and a few months later (one of the electors having had a change of heart), Alfonso X of Castile. Neither was so foolhardy as to take up permanent residence in Germany. Alfonso never set foot there while Richard made three visits to the Rhineland without ever establishing any effective control. Not until his death in 1273 did the election of Rudolph of Hapsburg initiate a new age and a new dynasty. Germany had been leaderless for more than twenty years.

THE LIFE OF GERTRUD

Gertrud of Helfta, born in 1256 on the Feast of the Epiphany, entered a turbulent society of which one historian wrote:

> Every floodgate of anarchy was opened: prelates and barons extended their domain by war: robber knights infested the highways and the rivers: the misery of the weak, the tyranny and violence of the strong, were such as had not been seen for centuries.[3]

Of Gertrud's family we know virtually nothing. From the fact that she became a choir-nun we may deduce that she was of noble, or at least gentle, birth. In Book I, Chapter 16 of *The Herald*, Christ is represented as saying, 'I banished her from all her relatives so that no one would love her on account of her connections: consequently I alone am the reason all her friends love her'.[4]

---

[3] J. Bryce, *The Holy Roman Empire* (London, 1910) 210.
[4] I, 16:5.

This implies that her family background was aristocratic and influential and under normal circumstances would have guaranteed
her respect and an honored place in society. It may also suggest
that she had in some sense been disowned or forgotten by her
relatives.

At the age of four she entered the monastery of Helfta, then
under the rule of Abbess Gertrud of Hackeborn. Child oblation
was still practised, even in the High Middle Ages, though one
feature of the cistercian reform had been its abolition. Strictly
speaking, cistercian monasteries accepted no one under the age of
fifteen and they kept no schools to educate the young unless they
were novices. But however widespread the practice may still have
been in other monastic circles, it is impossible not to feel some
curiosity at the reasons for Gertrud's apparent abandonment. That
she had not been rejected from birth but had had some experience,
which had made an ineradicable impression, of a happy home
life in a noble family, we may fairly deduce from a passage in
Book II, Chapter 18, in which Gertrud compares Christ to 'the
father of a family, who takes a real joy in the graceful poise of
his numerous children, on whom a vast crowd of relatives and
neighbors congratulate him. Among them he has a little child
who has not yet achieved the poise of the rest, but in his fatherly
love he feels sorry for it, clasps it to his bosom more often, and
spoils it more than the others with kind words and little presents'.[5]
The woman who described her religious experience in such terms
had surely once been a much-petted and adored youngest child,
and much of her imagery elsewhere is also taken from family
relationships.

Possibly Gertrud was one of the innocent victims of the chaos
of Germany in the 1250s, the inevitable concomitant of civil war
and anarchy, in the course of which her father may have suffered
death or disgrace. Or perhaps she was the victim of an unfortunate
second marriage, with an unsympathetic step-parent finding little
Trutta an awkward reminder of the past and Helfta a convenient
oubliette. On the other hand, she might well have been the precious
sacrificial offering of pious and devout parents.

[5]II, 18:1.

Gertrud passed the rest of her childhood in the monastery, where along with other girls she received a solid grounding in the liberal arts. In the thirteenth century this would certainly have included the *trivium*— grammar, rhetoric and dialectic—and perhaps the *quadrivium*—music, geometry, arithmetic and astronomy. The Helfta community was both learned and fervent. The ability to write highly rhetorical and florid Latin was considered nothing unusual. Gertrud herself writes fluently and easily; her biographer's style is less varied and flexible but still competent. Both women show a knowledge of the Latin fathers of the church— they cite Augustine, Gregory, Bernard, and the Victorines—and both are imbued through and through with the Latin phrases of the Vulgate and the liturgy.

Gertrud's early life was uneventful, though she makes much of her misspent youth. But her 'malice and wickedness' merely amounted, it seems, to a somewhat lukewarm and passive commitment to her vocation and an excessive devotion to her literary studies. In 1280, however, at the age of twenty-five, she underwent a conversion experience, the first of a series of visions which set her firmly on the mystic way and led her to abandon the liberal arts she loved so much for the study of theology. In this her progress is distinctively monastic: Dom Jean Leclercq has written of the 'two components of monastic culture: studies undertaken, and then, not precisely scorned, but renounced and transcended, for the sake of the kingdom of God'[6], an experience which repeats that of Saint Benedict himself. But Gertrud was also, however unconsciously, reflecting the usual educational practice of the Middle Ages, for at the universities the arts course was merely a prelude to higher studies in law, medicine or theology.

Gertrud's intellectual activities did not cease after her conversion: rather, they took a new direction. Her biographer sketches her work as a teacher and populariser, an exegete who rewrote complex passages in a simpler style (still, no doubt, in Latin), a compiler of extracts from the Fathers, and a composer of prayers and spiritual exercises. Above all she was a writer, and a writer of Latin, to an extent most unusual in a medieval woman

[6] *The Love of Learning and the Desire for God*, trans. C. Misrahi (New York, 1961) 15.

visionary. Like Saint Bernard she exercised *ministerium verbi*, the ministry of the word. Leclercq, who reminds us that 'the corrective for literature is the experience of God', has brilliantly captured the essence of her apostolate of learning in writing of the potential conflict and actual reconciliation between sanctity and learning:

> To combine a patiently acquired culture with a simplicity won through the power of fervent love, to keep simplicity of soul in the midst of the diverse attractions of the intellectual life, and, in order to accomplish this, to place oneself and remain firmly on the plane of the conscience, to raise knowledge to its level and never let it fall below: this is what the cultivated monk succeeds in doing. He is a scholar, he is versed in letters but he is not merely a man of science nor a man of letters nor an intellectual, he is a spiritual man.[7]

Gertrud is proof that there were women too in the Middle Ages who lived up to this monastic ideal.

The rest of her life was outwardly uneventful. Contrary to an earlier belief, which arose from confusion with Gertrud of Hackeborn, abbess of Helfta, she was never abbess nor, as far as we know, did she hold any official position in the community. Her life was filled with prayer, visions, writing, and spiritual direction. After much sickness she died about 1302.

For two centuries after her death, her autobiographical *Legatus divinae pietatis* was forgotten. Unlike the *Liber specialis gratiae*, which was probably also written by Gertrud, it was not translated into any of the medieval vernaculars. Five manuscripts survive, none earlier than the fifteenth century, but only two are complete. The provenance of two of the manuscripts is carthusian and it was in fact the carthusian monk Lanspergius, of the Cologne charterhouse, who was the first to publish Gertrud's writings in 1536. This edition was followed by a number of others in the sixteenth and seventeenth centuries, and also by translations, chiefly into French, as Gertrud began to emerge from a long period of oblivion.[8]

[7] *Ibid.*, 317.
[8] See Doyère, II:58–77.

GERTRUD IN HER TIME

Gertrud belongs, as we have seen, to the late thirteenth century, a period some regard as the zenith of the High Middle Ages and others as the beginning of its long decline. Compared to the twelfth century, the age that saw Cîteaux at its most influential and the cistercian writers at their most fertile and original, it has been described as 'at once more sober and more mature. . . . If it is less variegated than its predecessor it is more controlled; if it offers less profusion in its activities, they are better directed'.[9] It is significant that one can no longer speak of a unified culture in the West as one can in the twelfth century, when Bernard and the Cistercians, Peter Abelard, John of Salisbury, and the neo-platonists associated with the cathedral school at Chartres all belonged recognizably to the same milieu. By the thirteenth century that unity had split into a number of separate cultures, and this becomes clear when one reviews the names of some of Gertrud's contemporaries: Dante Alighieri (1265–1321), Meister Eckhart (1260– 1327), the philosophers Duns Scotus (1265–1308), Henry of Ghent (1217–1293), Giles of Rome (1247–1316) and the poet, philosopher, and archbishop John Peckham (1240–1292).

Gertrud seems hardly to belong to the same world as some of these distinguished men, particularly the philosophers who in the minds of many epitomize the thirteenth century, the age of the reception of Aristotle and the growth of the universities, dominated by dialectic and presiding with complacence over the decline of the other liberal arts. Rather Gertrud seems at least superficially to be a throw-back to the previous century, to be numbered in spirit with Bernard, Aelred of Rievaulx, and William of St Thierry. But this is not the whole story. We must remember the stable and continuing existence of a monastic culture unlike that of the secular schools. Leclercq has gone so far as to speak of 'two Middle Ages' coexisting:

> To be sure, the culture developed in the monastic Middle Ages differs from that developed in scholastic circles. The monastic

[9]Gordon Leff, *Medieval Thought* (London, 1958) 171.

> Middle Ages is essentially patristic because it is thoroughly pen-
> etrated by ancient sources and, under their influence, centred
> on the great realities which are at the very heart of Christian-
> ity.... Above all, it is based on biblical interpretation similar
> to the Fathers' and, like theirs, founded on reminiscence, the
> spontaneous recall of texts taken from Scripture itself.[10]

Gertrud is perhaps the leading female representative in the thirteenth century of this monastic culture: a writer and visionary
'literary rather than speculative' who came from an environment
where dialectic had not been allowed to grow at the expense of
its sister-arts, grammar and rhetoric.

Indeed for a woman there was simply no access to 'the other
Middle Ages', for the only entrance to the world of scholasticism
lay through the universities and *studia generalia* of the mendicant orders from which women were excluded. There could only be one
setting in which they had any chance of achieving their academic
and literary potential within the mainstream of medieval European
culture—a culture that was above all else a Latin culture—and that
was the cloister. The achievements of the nuns of Helfta show that
there were indeed some innately talented women who, given opportunity and a suitable education, could enter this culture as the
equals of men.

Gertrud was writing at a time when the vernacular was
coming into greater use, especially for religious writing. The
rich devotional literature produced by or for women outside the
cloister (whether they were anchorites, béguines or even lay-
women) invariably used the vernacular: Mechtild of Magdebourg
wrote in her native Low German; Meister Eckhart composed
his best-known works in High German; in England *Ancrene
Wisse* circulated in English and French. But there never seems
to have been any question of Gertrud writing in a vernacular
and her Latin is strongly Latinate, not at all the simple Latin
that indicates translation from, or composition in, another language. Ironically though this did not guarantee her writings the
diffusion through the pan-European culture of the medieval
Church which she might have expected, for the initiative was

---

[10] *The Love of Learning . . .*, 136.

passing from Latin to the vernaculars, and it took the invention of the printing press, the renaissance and the counter-reformation to launch Gertrud into a world which was by then very different.

THE HERALD

BOOK ONE

Book One was written by a nun of Helfta who had known Gertrud intimately and profited from her spiritual direction over many years. It fails to fall neatly into any precise literary *genre* as it is neither medieval hagiography nor modern biography. It is clearly designed to edify but avoids hackneyed motifs and refuses to pander to a taste for marvels. Its failure to conform to the conventions will immediately strike anyone familiar with medieval saints' lives. There are no pre-natal predictions of future sanctity, no quasi-miraculous nativity scenes, no childhood anecdotes pointing to a precocious holiness. Indeed, there is nothing at all about Gertrud's birth, family background, or life before she entered the monastery. There are no youthful struggles against the temptations of the flesh (a passionate absorption in one's education is inevitably unsensational), nor do we find later any accounts of miraculous cures, the most common type of miracle in medieval hagiography. There is no account of an edifying death-bed scene, apparitions to others after death, or miracles performed at the saint's tomb. Book One has nothing to say of Gertrud's death, though Book Five includes an account of death-bed graces and consolations. In short, Book One impresses the reader with its sincerity and sobriety.

But it is not a biography in the modern sense. Chapter One is the only part of the book to rely on a chronological structure. The writer, who was clearly a conscious artist and perhaps a little proud of her stately and ornate Latinity, was by the uneventful nature of Gertrud's life denied any framework based on a sequence of events, and instead composed an eulogistic memoir on which she imposed a purely rhetorical structure. Modern readers may well find this structure irritatingly over-ingenious, not to say precious, but it is a brave attempt to prevent her essay degenerating into a mere concatenation of edifying recollections.

Chapters Two, Three and Four are based on the conceit that all statements in a court of law, according to the Old Testament, had to be sustantiated by two or three witnesses. Seeking a favorable verdict on Gertrud's claim to sanctity, her biographer calls as her first witness God himself and in Chapter Two records the evidence of divine Providence as to Gertrud's special status: two examples of precognition and two of her ability to release others from temptation. The second witness consists of a group of people (mainly other nuns of Helfta) who were granted revelations touching on Gertrud's sanctity: Chapter Three reveals much about the spiritual climate of Helfta, apparently a veritable nest of visionaries, where many of the nuns received private revelations and communicated them to each other. The third witness is the saint's own life and Chapter Four particularly stresses her complete devotion to God's glory, her humility and absence of self-seeking, and her generosity in sharing her spiritual experiences.

Having exhausted the possibilities of the courtroom conceit, the writer then bases her next seven chapters on a passage from one of Saint Bernard's sermons on the Song of Songs that compares the soul of a saint, as God's dwelling-place, with a heaven in which are set various virtues as the sun, the moon and the stars. The sun is Gertrud's integrity, her passion for souls, and her sympathy with those in distress; the moon is her chastity; the stars her many other virtues. The writer goes on to invoke Scripture to extend the simile beyond Bernard's sketch: heaven not only has its planets and stars, it also produces thunder, lightning and dew. Gertrud's thunder was her outspoken denunciation of sin, her dew the grace of God she mediated and the tears of compunction she elicited, her lightning the miracles she performed. As a pendant in Chapter Fourteen the writer enumerates the special privileges granted Gertrud by God, particularly in discerning the dispositions of those who wished to receive communion.

The subsequent chapters are effectively appendices. They comprise an account of the circumstances of the writing of Book Two; an expansion of Chapter Five recording further revelations granted to others that confirm the authenticity of her special privileges; and a prophecy of the even more complete union with God for which she is destined. Finally Chapter Seventeen rounds off the book with a brief account of her later spiritual development.

As there is no mention of Gertrud's death Book One was possibly written toward the end of her life but before she had died.

Such a summary inevitably highlights the literary artifice of Book One. But closer acquaintance reveals an interesting text. An account by one woman of another is rare in the Middle Ages — though another example is Elsbet Stagel's early-fourteenth century account of the lives of the Dominican sisters of Toess — and for all its panegyric purpose this is an authentic portrait of a real live woman. It does not invariably single out for comment those virtues that so often construct the medieval stereotype of a holy woman. Gertrud emerges as passionate in her thirst for others' conversions and in her devotion to the religious life (in this she reminds one of Saint Bernard); as endowed with a child-like trust in God's mercy, but at the same time fully adult in her integrity and her refusal to put anyone or anything before the absolute demands of God. Above all she is praised for *libertas cordis*, 'nobility of heart', a single-minded detachment and independence.

The emphasis on this virtue raises the possibility of a connection between Book One and the teachings of Meister Eckhart in his 'Talks of Instruction'. These were probably composed shortly before 1298, when Eckhart was in Thuringia, the duchy within which Helfta was situated. At that time Helfta was under the spiritual direction of the Dominicans and Eckhart was himself a Friar Preacher. In his 'Talks' he speaks of the power of a 'free mind', by which he seems to have meant just that *libertas* the author of Book One praises in Gertrud. Eckhart is often conceived as one of a generation who came after Gertrud, a neo-plotinian mystic of a type alien to Gertrud's visionary christocentric mysticism. But they were close contemporaries and Eckhart was actually Vicar of Thuringia and Prior of Erfurt toward the end of the thirteenth century. It seems strange that points of contact between the two have never been investigated. A few parallels (indicated in the Notes) do suggest that the author of Book One, if not Gertrud herself, had come into contact with some of Eckhart's more orthodox ideas.

Gertrud is inevitably praised for her chastity, but this virtue does not receive the emphasis usually placed upon it in accounts of medieval women saints. If her modesty seems excessive to modern readers they should bear in mind that she had lived as long as she could remember in a totally female environment. Men must have seemed strange and alien creatures indeed. Moreover even at Helfta her modesty was a family joke: 'Her close friends used sometimes to say that she should rightly be put on the altar among the relics, because of the purity of her heart'.[11] Her biographer emphasises the positive nature of her chastity, which was nourished by constant study and meditative reading of Scripture rather than by physical mortifications. Such mortifications are conspicuous by their absence throughout Books One and Two: Gertrud seems never to have sought out physical suffering though she accepted her greater than average share, as she perceived that it played a valuable part in preparing her soul for mystical graces.

But her virtues are not the only subject of Book One. We learn of major faults, often confirmed by Gertrud herself in Book Two. Sometimes she spoke out against sin too boldly, too harshly, at least for the taste of one sister, herself a visionary.[12] She was impulsive and restless, and tended to leave tasks unfinished (no doubt she overcommitted herself). She herself thought she lacked the particularly feminine virtues of gentleness and patience and she easily gave way to anger.[13] In a revealing moment she accuses herself of talking too much, thus manifesting a degree of self-knowledge unusual even in a saint.[14]

Finally, Book One indicates her many spiritual gifts. Apart from visions and locutions, she experienced an invisible stigmata and what are known as 'signs of espousal'; she showed a super-natural knowledge of events distant in time and space; her prayers were extraordinarily efficacious. But more than anything else the stress falls on her talents in the quasi-sacerdotal role of spiritual director, especially on her powers of discernment. Little is made of her 'miracles' —her infallible ability to find a needle in a haystack is the most memorable[15]—and it is unlikely that those few that are recounted would survive the rigors of a modern canonization process. Gertrud was no wonder-worker: her true miracles were

[11]I, 9:1.
[12]I,12:1.
[13]I,16:4.
[14]II, 20:5.
[15]1, 13:4.

the transformations of others for which she prepared the way by her words, spoken or written.

BOOK TWO

Book Two must inevitably overshadow, not only Book One but also the remaining three books of *The Herald*, as it alone comes directly from the pen of Gertrud. It is the original account of her spiritual experiences and is best left to speak for itself. But as Gertrud is often regarded as pivotal in the growth of devotion to the Sacred Heart, a brief attempt is here made to indicate her importance in this respect.

It is ironic that one of the few medieval women to whom posterity has given the epithet 'the Great' is known to the world, if at all, merely as the precursor of Jean Eudes and Margaret Mary Alacoque. This at least recognizes that devotion to the Heart of Jesus was not a post-reformation seventeenth-century innovation but was known to the Middle Ages. In its earliest days it was closely connected with the cistercian movement and it has often been emphasised that such a cult would have been impossible without that tender devotion to Christ's humanity which we associate with Saint Bernard and cistercian spirituality in general. Devotion to the Heart of Jesus was originally an extension of devotion to the Five Wounds, specifically to the Wound in the Side, as an influential passage from Sermon 61.4 of Bernard's *Sermons on the Song of Songs* makes clear:

> The ark of his heart is laid open through the clefts of his body:
> that mighty mystery of loving-kindness is laid open, laid open
> too the tender mercies of our God, in which the morning star
> from on high has risen upon us.[16]

Here Bernard contemplates, through that wound, the 'ark of the heart' that symbolizes God's *pietas*. William of St Thierry (1080–1148), Bernard's contemporary, fellow Cistercian, and one of his closest friends, also hails Christ's Heart under the type of the ark of the covenant; while Richard of St Victor (d. 1173), in

[16]SC 61:4.

the peroration to his treatise *De Emmanuele*, praises the sweetness of that Heart, which surpasses all things.[17]

In the first half of the thirteenth century the incipient devotion moved out of the writings of mystical theologians into the experiences of women visionaries, particularly in the Low Countries. The first person to receive a supernatural private revelation of the Heart of Jesus seems to have been the Flemish visionary Lutgarde of Aywières. Lutgarde was a very different type of mystic from Gertrud and we are dependent for our knowledge of her on Thomas of Cantimpré, OP (c. 1200–1250), a somewhat credulous writer primarily interested in miracles and physical phenomena who also wrote a life of Christina Mirabilis. But even he found too much some of the visions Lutgarde related to him and refused to record them.

Lutgarde was born c. 1182, entered the benedictine monastery of Saint Trond as a child and had a sentimental affair with a young man from which she was converted at the age of fifteen or sixteen by a vision of Christ uncovering his wounded heart. She subsequently entered the cistercian abbey at Aywières. Later she claimed that an exchange of hearts had taken place and she developed above her own heart a bleeding wound, the scar of which remained until she died in 1246, ten years before Gertrud was born. Other visionaries connected with the devotion lived around the same time in the same area: Hadewijch the béguine and Beatrice of Nazareth (c.1205–1268), another cistercian nun, whose heart was mystically pierced by a flaming arrow.[18]

References to the Heart of Jesus are also to be found in late thirteenth-century poetry. The English poet John Howden (c. 1272), who wrote mystical poetry in Latin and was 'one of the major religious poets in the Middle Ages'[19], manifests a devotion to the Heart in his lengthy poem on the Passion, *Philomena*.[20] He wrote of the Heart of Jesus pierced by the sword of love in

[17]PL 196:655.
[18]See Debognie, 153–9.
[19]F.J.E. Raby, *A History of Christian-Latin Poetry* (Oxford, 2nd. ed.1953) 389.
[20]Ed. C. Blüme, *Hymnologische Beiträge* IV (1930).

the Garden of Gethsemane[21], and one section of seventeen stanzas greets *pectus et Cor Jesu* as the tabernacle (*sacrarium*) of Love, as eyrie or nest (*aerarium*), as the divine wine-cellar, source of mercy and fount of wisdom, throne of charity, and the shrine or reliquary of godhead (*Deitatis. .. scrinium*). The Heart calls to mind the traditional image of the pelican that pierces its breast to feed its young with its own blood, and Christ's Heart, on which Love has written, surpasses the faithful heart of the turtle-dove.[22] Howden's extravagant imagery of flowers, sweetness, and spring is curiously reminiscent of Gertrud's and raises the intriguing possibility of contact or influence. In fact he was chaplain to Eleanor, wife of Henry III, whose younger brother, Richard of Cornwall, was King of the Romans and made three expeditions to Germany before his death in 1273.

Contemporary with Gertrud herself were the Italian visionaries Angela of Foligno (1249–1309) and Margaret of Cortone (1247–1297), who both received visions of the Heart. But in the late-thirteenth century the monastery of Helfta decisively seized the leadership of the incipient movement. Besides Gertrud herself Helfta sheltered Mechtild of Magdebourg (1220–1282), a béguine who came for refuge late in life in 1270 and the extent of whose influence on Gertrud is disputed (a few parallels are given in the Notes). Although her writings are quite different from Gertrud's (she knew no Latin and composed *The Flowing Light of the Godhead* in her mother tongue) some of the visions she relates mention the Heart of Jesus.[23]

Mechtild of Magdebourg is not to be confused with Saint Mechtild of Hackeborn (1241–c.1298), to whom *The Herald* always refers as 'Dame M. of blessed memory' or 'Dame M. the chantress' (in this translation always expanded as 'M[echtild]'). She was the younger sister of the great abbess, Gertrud of Hackeborn (1231–1292), under whose rule Gertrud herself spent most of her life, and was mistress of novices and later Gertrud's close friend

[21]Stanza 98.

[22]Stanzas 213–229.

[23]English translation by Lucy Menzies, *The Revelations of Mechthild of Magdeborg, 1210–1297: The Flowing Light of the Godhead* (London, 1953).

and spiritual confidante. The *Liber specialis gratiae*[24], a record of Mechtild's visionary experiences in which the Heart is as prominent as in Gertrud's own revelations, was almost certainly compiled by the latter in the years before Mechtild's death.

This traditional view of Gertrud as taking her place, prominent though it may be, in a line of mystical writers and visionaries headed by Saint Bernard and culminating in Margaret Mary Alacoque[25] has the disadvantage of tying her firmly to a devotion to the Sacred Heart which has had its period of popularity but is now identified by many with bad art, mawkish sentimentality, and the pre-Vatican II, pre-*aggiornamento*, days of the Roman Catholic Church. Such an approach does Gertrud an injustice. It is preferable to consider what exactly the Heart of Jesus meant to her, in her own time, and to attempt to explicate her spirituality without reference to later developments which really have nothing to do with her and neither derive from nor find any justification in her writings. She herself never used the collocation *cor sacrum*, and the divinely-sanctioned title of her book makes no mention of the Heart. Indeed it is that title, *Legatus divinae pietatis*, which provides the vital clue to an understanding of the saint's message. Gertrud should be seen, not so much as the apostle of the Sacred Heart as of the divine *pietas*, of which the Heart is the living embodiment. Hence it is seen not as a suffering heart in need of consolation and reparation, but as the loving and nurturing heart of the risen and triumphant Christ.

The connotations of *pietas* are naturally important. The word has an interesting and chequered history and its classical Latin meanings range widely. Primarily it signifies the attitude of dutiful respect toward those to whom one is bound by ties of religion and consanguinity: this includes the attitude of human beings to the gods and, more rarely, the reciprocal attitude of the gods; the affection of child for parent and parent for child; the love between spouses; and finally the attitude of citizens to the state and of

[24]*Revelationes Gertrudianae et Mechtildianae*, 2 vols., ed. Benedictines of Solesmes (Poitier and Paris, 1875–77); see also Theresa A. Halligan, ed., *The Book of Gostlye Grace of Mechtild of Hackeborn* (Toronto, 1979).

[25]For an excellent account to which I am greatly indebted see Debognie.

soldiers toward their commanding officer.[26] In the Middle Ages the word, when used of God, is extended to mean mercy and compassion.[27] The one common factor is that *pietas* springs not from the passions but from some objectively-perceived relationship existing between unequals.

In Gertrud's writings *pietas* signifies the attitude of loving concern that God shows toward all people, not exclusively toward souls favored with extraordinary supernatural experiences. It includes mercy, not the chilly clemency of a distant ruler toward his subjects but the compassionate affection of a father for his children. In this translation it is rendered throughout as 'loving-kindness' though it could be as accurately if more clumsily translated as 'the parental love of the deity'. In this connection we may note that although Gertrud often uses the traditional mystical image of the soul as the spouse of Christ, she just as often uses the image of parent and child when speaking of the Lord's dealings with her soul.

The author of Book One sees the proclamation of this loving concern as Gertrud's divinely-ordained mission: 'God chose her . . . to make known through her the mysteries of his *pietas*.'[28] It was her comprehensive grasp of those mysteries that provided the foundation for the 'sure trust in God's kindly mercy',[29] which her biographer singles out for special mention. This all-pervading trust underlay her rejection of formalism in religion. For instance, we are told that she was willing to die without the last rites because she was convinced that whether she died a long-foreseen or sudden death (a fate universally regarded in the Middle Ages with profound horror), it would be divinely ordained to ensure her salvation.[30] Similarly, she never allowed the fact that she had not carried out particular preparatory devotions to prevent her from receiving communion. Indeed, trusting in the divine loving-kindness, she was a great advocate of frequent communion and sometimes almost dragged to the altar her scrupulous sisters who dwelt overmuch on their unworthiness.

[26]See *Oxford Latin Dictionary s. v.* PIETAS.
[27]See R.E.Latham, ed., *Revised Medieval Word List* (London, 1965).
[28]I, 2:2.
[29]I, 10:1.
[30]I, 10:4.

Gertrud's adoption of the same Old Testament 'type' of the Heart—the ark of the covenant—as that used by Bernard and William of St Thierry, suggests another facet of her spirituality. The Heart is the dwelling-place of *deitas*, of Christ's godhead or divine nature, and she greets the Lord's breast as 'that treasury in which the fullness of the divine dwells bodily' (*corporaliter*).[31] Elsewhere she speaks of 'that most noble ark of godhead, your deified Heart'.[32] Her devotion to the Heart thus becomes an affirmation of Christ's divinity; but as that heart is a living and beating heart that no purely spiritual being could possess, it is simultaneously an assertion of Christ's true, perfect and complete humanity. Gertrud therefore speaks to us of the two natures of Christ, fused through the mystery of the incarnation.

The supernatural heat of Christ's heart manifests its *deitas* but also its warmth of human affection. The 'molten core'[33] is the source of an ardor which both consumes and transforms. The Heart is 'a devastating glowing coal', a 'truly devouring fire', a 'powerful furnace'.[34] Its heat is presented most strikingly in Book Two, Chapter Eight, where she sees the Heart continuously producing and then reabsorbing tiny droplets of sweat.[35] But paradoxically it is also a place of sweet repose and Gertrud greets it as 'eternal solstice, safe dwelling'.[36]

One should also mention the important part played by Gertrud's own heart. It is there that she receives, 'as if in physical places' (*intus in corde meo quasi in corporalibus locis*)[37] the imprint of Christ's wounds for which she had prayed and, later, a wound from an arrow proceeding from Christ's own wounded heart.[38] It is clear, incidentally, from the purely symbolic way in which Gertrud treats these 'wounds', by washing them with devotion, salving them with thanksgiving, and binding them up with integrity, that

[31]II, 7:1.
[32]II, 23:8.
[33]II, 19:1.
[34]II, 7:2.
[35]II, 8:4.
[36]II, 8:5.
[37]II, 4:3.
[38]II, 5:2.

they have no physical manifestations. In general Gertrud's vision-ary experiences seem to be primarily symbolic or emblematic: they are strongly visual but the imaginative image is always subor-dinated to an extensive and throrough verbal interpretation.

But some readers may come to suspect that for Gertrud the Heart held other resonances, not so much theological as psychological. At times the Lord implicitly speaks of himself as Gertrud's mother: 'From her childhood I have borne and carried her in my embrace'[39]; her heart, united with his, beats in har-mony with it: 'The beatings of her heart are unceasingly mingled with the beatings of my love . . . . But I am holding back the full force of my own heart-beats until the hour of her death'.[40] This enclosure of Gertrud within Christ's glorified body, a mystical union described so beautifully if strangely by these images, finds its closest human analogy in the child's dimly-remembered uterine experience of its mother's heart-beats that constantly soothe and reassure. The heart is indeed 'a safe dwelling' and 'the promised land'. If Gertrud can convey to us something of the parental love of God, a love maternal as well as paternal, that subsumes and transcends gender, then perhaps she has a message for those in the late-twentieth century who hope to see theological thought and language liberated from outmoded patriarchal constraints.

Alexandra Barratt

University of Waikato
Hamilton, New Zealand

[39]I, 3:6.
[40]I, 3:4.

TRANSLATOR'S NOTE

THE AUTHOR OF BOOK ONE never refers to Gertrud by name.
As this is a significant and interesting feature of her style it
has been preserved in the translation but occasionally in the
interests of clarity Gertrud's name has been added in square brackets. On a very few other occasions where it has been necessary to
add to the text, those additions are also in square brackets.

I should like to thank Brother John Leinenweber of the Her-
mitage of the Dayspring, who revised the text and made many
helpful corrections and suggestions. Those inaccuracies and infe-
licities that remain are my own responsibility.

A.B.

EDITOR'S NOTE

The editors of Cistercian Publications join with Dr. Barratt
in thanking Brother John Leinenweber for his invaluable editorial
help in preparing this manuscript for publication, and wish to
express their appreciation to Professor Gertrud Jaron Lewis and
Ron Kastner for their advice.

ENDORSEMENT AND AUTHORIZATION

IN THE YEAR OF OUR LORD 1289, God's abundant grace inspired the initial writing of this book. Afterwards, on the initiative of the monastic superiors, it was examined and approved by distinguished theologians, friars of the Orders of Preachers and Minors.[1] It was first read and approved by the scholarly Brother H. of Mulhausen,[2] a man filled with the Holy Spirit, and also by Brother H. of Weriungerode[3] when he was at the house in Halle. It was then given full approval by the brother known as 'of Burch' who was lecturer to the Friars Minor at the Halberstadt convent around AD 1300. He was highly distinguished both for his literary achievements and for his special gift of spiritual balm. It was then examined in greater detail by Brother Nicolaus, lecturer at Hildesheim, who around AD 1301 was prior at Halberstadt. Brother Theodoricus, too, known as 'of Apoldia',[4] held frequent conversations with the author and gave his complete approval to her discourses and their general import. Also Dom Gotfried Fex, a master[5] of tested ability, was fired by this person's words with so great an enthusiasm for God's will that from then onwards he happily spent his whole life in wonderful devotion and longing for God. Similarly Brother Herman, known as 'of Loweia', a lecturer of the Order of Preachers at Leipzig, and many other members of

[1]That is, the Dominicans and Franciscans.
[2]Now Muhlhausen.
[3]Now Wernigerode.
[4]Now Apolda.
[5]Holder of a master's degree and therefore a university teacher.

29

the same order who are worthy of belief, on hearing her words vouched for her unreservedly on God's behalf. Someone else who had read through this book and examined it with considerable care wrote as follows:

> I declare in the very truth of the divine light that no one who truly possesses the Holy Spirit may have the audacious temerity to object to these writings in any way. Rather, strengthened by the spirit of the one and only Lover of humankind, a spirit that cannot lie, I bind myself to fight to the death on behalf of these writings against anyone, whoever he may be.

PROLOGUE

THE SPIRIT PARACLETE, DISPENSER of all good things, who breathes where he wills,[1] as he wills, and when he wills, seeks (as is most fitting) to keep his inbreathings secret. Yet for the salvation of many he also ordains a fitting way of bringing his inbreathings to light, as is clear in this handmaid of God. Although the vast flood of God's loving-kindness never ceased to flow into her without pause, he nonetheless ordained a pause before it flowed out. So it was that this book was written down at various times, one part written down eight years after her reception of grace, and the second part completed about twenty years later.

2. Each time the Lord graciously declared that he found both parts welcome. For when the first part had been written and she had commended it to the Lord with humble devotion, she received this reply from God's most generous loving-kindness: 'No one can take from me the memorial of the abundance of my divine sweetness'.[2] She understood by these words that the Lord wanted to have the little book entitled *A memorial of the abundance of the divine sweetness.* And the Lord added, 'If anyone wishes to read this book with a devout intention of spiritual progress, I shall draw him so closely to myself that he will read it as if my own hands were holding the book and I myself shall keep him company at the task. As when two people are reading the same page, each is aware of the other's breath, so shall I draw in the breath of his longings. This

[1] Jn 3:8.
[2] Ps 144:7 / 145:7.

31

shall move my loving-kindness to have mercy on him.[3] Moreover I shall breathe into him the breath of my divinity which, through my Spirit, will create him anew within'. The Lord also added, 'If anyone transcribes what is written here with a similar intention, for every single word I shall fire at him, from the sweetness of my divine heart, an arrow of love which will set in motion in his soul the most delightful pleasures of divine goodness'.

3. While the second part was being written, which also soothed God's will greatly, and she was complaining to the Lord one night, he soothed her with his wonted kindness and said, among other things, 'I have given you as a light for the nations, that you may be my salvation from the uttermost ends of the earth'.[4] When she understood that he was speaking of this book, which at the time had scarcely been started, she said in astonishment, 'And how, God, can anyone be enlightened by means of this little book when it is not my intention to write any more and I shall certainly not allow even what little I have already written to be made public?' The Lord replied, 'When I chose Jeremiah to be a prophet he thought he did not know how to speak[5] and that he lacked the necessary powers of discernment; but by means of his eloquence I brought nations and kingdoms back to the right path. In the same way, whatever I have arranged to illuminate through you by the light of knowledge and truth will not be frustrated, for no one can thwart my eternally predestined plan. I shall call those whom I have predestined, and I shal justify those whom I have called,[6] in any way that pleases me'.

4. Another time, while she was again struggling in prayer to win from the Lord the promise that he would allow her to prevent the writing of this book, because at that time obedience to her superiors was not compelling her to write as insistently as it had earlier, the Lord graciously replied, 'Do you not know that anyone whom my will compels is compelled by a force greater than any

[3]Gn 43:30.
[4]Is 49:6.
[5]Jer 1:6.
[6]Rm 8:30.

obedience? Since, then, you know that it is my will, which no one can resist,[7] that this book should be written, why are you perturbed? I both urge you to undertake its writing and shall faithfully assist you; and what is my own I shall keep unharmed'.

Then she, conforming her entire will to the divine pleasure, said to the Lord, 'What title do you want this book to have, most loving Lord?' The Lord replied, 'This book of mine will be called *The herald of the divine loving-kindness*, for some of the overflowing abundance of my loving-kindness will spill over into it'. She was very surprised at this and said, 'Since those people who are called heralds enjoy considerable authority, what authority do you condescend to grant this little book by giving it that name?' The Lord replied, 'By virtue of my divinity I grant this, that anyone who reads it to praise me with correct faith, humble devotion and religious gratitude, and who seeks to be edified, may receive remission of venial sins and will obtain the gift of spiritual consolation and will, moreover, become capable of more ample graces'.

5. Afterwards, realizing that the Lord wanted the two parts combined into one, she asked him in devout prayer how they should be blended, as he had condescended to distinguish between them, giving them separate titles as I recorded earlier. The Lord replied, 'Just as the birth of a lovely child sometimes leads each of its parents to look on the other more affectionately, so I have preordained that this book should result from a union of both parts and the title emerge from both, that is, *The Herald: A memorial of the abundance of the divine loving-kindness*, for it will herald my loving-kindness in the memory of those that I have chosen'.

6. Since it will become clear from what follows that she constantly enjoyed the presence of the divine generosity, and yet she sometimes inserted 'he appeared', or 'the Lord was with her', this must be understood to mean that although he was indeed often with her, by a special privilege, nonetheless there were periods when for some reason or some time he appeared to her in a form more amenable to the imagination, in conformity with the capacity of those around her, to whom he preordained that a particular revelation should be communicated. Similarly it is also essential to

[7]Introit formerly used on the twenty-first Sunday after Pentecost, adapted from Est 13:9.

know, in regard to the varied material that follows, that God, the lover of all that exists, in visiting one seeks in different ways the salvation of many. And although the loving Lord, on both ordinary and feast days, continuously and impartially poured out his grace on her, through visions of physical likenesses as well as through purer enlightenments of her thoughts, all the same he wished to have described in this little book visions of physical likenesses, for human understanding. Thus it is divided into five parts to suit the powers of discernment and abilities of those who read it.

7. The first part contains commendations of her character and testimonies to her grace. The second book contains what she herself recorded, as an act of thanksgiving, at the instigation of God's Spirit, concerning how she received this grace. The third book expounds something of the favors lavished on or revealed to her; the fourth records the visitations by which the divine loving-kindness consoled her on certain feast-days. Then the fifth book expresses something of what the Lord condescended to reveal to her on the merits of departed souls. It also adds something of the consolations which the Lord condescended to advance to her just before her death.

8. But as Hugh says, 'I hold suspect all truth which is not confirmed by scriptural authority', and again, 'No revelation, however truthful it appears, should be endorsed without the witness of Moses and Elijah, that is, without the authority of Scripture'[8], I have therefore recorded in the margin what my simple wit and inexperienced understanding could recall on the spur of the moment, in the hope that if anyone of keener wit and more experienced understanding should come across it, he would be able to cite far more credible and appropriate witnesses.

[8]Richard of St Victor, *Benjamin Minor* 81; PL 196:57. This work was frequently attributed to Hugh of St Victor in the Middle Ages.

BOOK ONE

CHAPTER ONE

IN COMMENDATION
OF HER CHARACTER

O THE DEPTHS OF THE RICHES OF THE WISDOM and knowledge of God: how unsearchable are his judgements, and his ways past finding out![1] In how many wonderful, hidden and diverse ways does he call those whom he has predestined, and graciously justify those whom he has called[2]—or rather, how justly he graces them and, as if he found them already justified, judges them worthy partners in all his riches and delights. All this is made manifest in this his chosen woman, whom he graciously planted like a dazzling white lily in the garden of the Church, amidst a bed of spices,[3] that is, in the company of the righteous.

When she was a little girl, less than five years old, he set her apart from the hustle and bustle of the world and called her to the wedding-chamber of the religious life. To her dazzling whiteness he so lavishly added the springtide beauty of every kind of flower that, graceful in the eyes of all,[4] she inclined the souls of many

[1]Rm 11:33.
[2]Rm 8:30; cf. Prologue.
[3]Sg 6:1.
[4]Est 2:15.

to love her. She was indeed tender in years and body, but in her perceptiveness old and wise: lovable, quick, articulate, and so consistently easy to teach that all those who heard her were astonished.

When she started school she was distinguished by such quickness of perception and such natural understanding that she outstripped all her contemporaries and other companions in all wisdom and instruction. In this way she passed the years of childhood and youth with a pure heart and an eager delight in the liberal arts, shielded by the Father of mercies[5] from the many childish aberrations that often occur at that age. For that, let us give him thanks and infinite praise.

2. But it pleased him who had set her apart from her mother's womb[6] and had despatched her, scarcely weaned, to the banquetting hall[7] of the monastic order, to call her by his grace from outward to inward preoccupations, from physical exercises to spiritual endeavors. This he accomplished by means of a clear revelation, as will become plain from what follows. From it she then realized that she had been far from God, in a land of unlikeness,[8] for while clinging too closely to the liberal arts, she had until that moment failed to adjust the eye of her mind to the light of spiritual understanding. By attaching herself too eagerly to the pleasure of human wisdom, she had deprived herself of the most delightful taste of true Wisdom. All outward things now suddenly seemed worthless to her, and rightly so, for the Lord then led her into a place of joy and gladness, to Mount Sion, that is, to the vision of himself. There she put off her old nature with its deeds and put

[5] 2 Cor 1:3.
[6] Gal 1:15.

[7] *triclinium*, a rare word, later (Bk II, 23.6) used to refer to the palace of Assuerus. In classical Latin it means the couch on which diners reclined and by extension the room where they dined. Possibly the redactor of Bk I was prompted to use the metaphor having just mentioned that Gertrude was 'scarcely weaned' (probably not mere rhetorical hyperbole).

[8] *regio dissimilitudinis*, a favorite phrase of St Bernard and his contemporaries. See E.H. Gilson, *The Mystical Theology of Saint Bernard*, trans. by A.H.C. Downes (London, 1940), *passim*.

on the new nature which is created after God's likeness in true
righteousness and holiness.[9]

No longer a student of literature, then, she became a student of theology and tirelessly ruminated on all the books of the
Bible which she could obtain. The basket of her heart she packed
to the very top with the more useful, and honey-sweet, texts of
holy Scripture, so that she always had at hand an instructive and
holy quotation. Hence she could give a ready and suitable answer
to anyone who came to her, and turn aside any kind of error
with scriptural witnesses so appropriate that almost no one could
refute her.

And in those days she was not sated by the wonderful sweetness
and the extraordinary pleasure of constant application to divine
contemplation or to the careful reading of holy Scripture. To her
it seemed honeycomb in the mouth, harmonious music in the
ear, and spiritual joy in the heart.[10] Elucidating and clarifying
what lesser minds found obscure, she made compilations from
the sayings of the saints, gathered as a dove gathers grain, and
committed to writing many books filled with all sweetness, for
the general profit of all those who wished to read them. She
also composed many prayers, 'sweeter than the honeycomb',[11]
and many other examples of spiritual exercises, in a style so fitting
that it was impossible for any authority[12] to find fault with it, or
do anything except delight in its aptness, which was founded on
such honeyed texts from holy Scripture that no one, theologian
or believer, could scorn it. This must be ascribed, there can be no
dispute, to the gift of spiritual grace.

But since some [of these characteristics] recorded above are
customarily praised among us for non-spiritual reasons—and as
Scripture says in the book of wisdom 'Grace is deceitful and beauty

---

[9]Eph 4:22–24

[10]The Latin recalls the lines of the cistercian poem *Dulcis Jesu memoriam*:

> Jesus decus angelicum,
> in aure dulce canticum
> in ore mel mirificum,
> cordi pigmentum caelicum.

[11]Ps 18:11/19:11.

[12]*nulli magistrorum.*

is vain: the woman that fears the Lord shall be praised'[13]—let us
also add those qualities which should rightly be praised.

3. She was a most strong pillar of the religious life, a most steadfast
champion of justice and truth, so what is said in the book of
wisdom about Simon the High Priest could fairly be said of her,
that 'during his life he was the prop and stay of the house' of the
religious life, 'and in his days he fortified the temple'[14] of spiritual
devotion; that is, her admonitions and example greatly encouraged
in many people a zealous striving for greater devotion. Yet it could
be said of her that in her day 'the wells of water poured out' and
so forth,[15] for in fact no one in our day has produced in greater
profusion than she the floods of that instruction which leads to
salvation.

She also possessed a sweet and piercing eloquence, an articulate
tongue, and speech so persuasive, effective and gracious that most
of those who heard her words testified, by the miraculous softening
of their hearts and the change in their wills, that God's spirit was
speaking in her.[16] It was the Word—living, effectual and sharper
than any two-edged sword, piercing to the division of the soul
and the spirit[17]—dwelling in her, which did all this. Some she
goaded by her words to salvation, others she enabled to see both
God and their own shortcomings; to some she brought the help of
consoling grace, and the hearts of others she caused to burn more
brightly with divine love. A large number, even of outsiders, who
had heard no more than a single utterance of hers, declared that
they had received great consolation from it. And although she was
generously endowed with these and similar gifts, which are usually
a source of human satisfaction, we must never think that she had
imagined what follows out of her wit or intellectual quickness to
please herself, or that she wrote it down because of her concern
for literary composition or skill in rhetoric. God forbid! Rather
we must firmly believe, without any hesitation, that the Spirit—

[13]Pr 31:30.
[14]Si 50:1.
[15]Cf. Pr 5:15.
[16]Ac 6:10.
[17]Heb 4:12.

who breathes where he wills,[18] when he wills, on whom he wills, and what he wills as befits the subject, the place and the time— poured out all this on her as a free gift from the very fountainhead of divine wisdom.

4. Since the unseen and the spiritual can never be expressed for human understanding other than through analogy with the physical and the visible, we have to suggest them by means of human and material images. Master Hugh attests this in his discourse *On the Inner Man*, Chapter Sixteen: 'Holy Scripture, in order to engage the speculative powers of lower beings, and to come down to the level of human frailty, describes invisible reality by means of the forms of visible things, and impresses their memory on our minds by the beauty of outward forms which arouse our desire. This is why it speaks sometimes of a land flowing with milk and honey, sometimes of flowers, sometimes of perfumes; sometimes the singing of people, the chorus of birds, symbolize the harmony of celestial joys'. Read the Revelation of John and you will find Jerusalem variously described as decorated with gold and silver and pearls, and various other gems. We know, of course, that none of them is there where, all the same, nothing can be altogether lacking, for nothing of that kind is there by substance,[19] but all of them are present by analogy.'[20]

18Jn 3:8; cf. Prologue, 1.
19*per speciem.*
20*per similitudinem.*

CHAPTER TWO

THE EVIDENCE OF GRACE

1. To the Lord God, giver of all true goods, let all that the circle of the skies,[1] the compass of the land and the depths of the abyss enclose, render thanks. Let them chant his praise—eternal, vast, immutable—which, proceeding from uncreated Love, achieves its greatest perfection in God himself, as the overflowing abundance of his loving-kindness.[2] Cascading into the valley of human weakness, this loving-kindness bent its gaze on this woman among others, charmed by the gift it had itself bestowed.

2. As Scripture reveals that all evidence depends on the words of two or three witnesses[3] and since there are a large number of witnesses available, we cannot dispute that God chose her as a kind of special instrument, to make known through her the mysteries of his loving-kindness.

The first and principal witness is God. Again and again he fulfilled her predictions and made known to all her secret insights. He allowed many people to experience the power of her prayers, or rather, he listened to their requests because of her merits; he even freed from temptation those who sought her help with a

[1]Introit for the twenty-first Sunday after Pentecost, adapted from Est 13:10.
[2]Collect for the eleventh Sunday after Pentecost.
[3]Dt 19:15; Mt 18:16.

42

faithful and a humble heart. I shall give a few examples from among many.

3. Once, at the time of the death of Rudolph, king of the Romans, she with others was praying for the election of his successor. On the very day and, we believe, even at the hour at which the election took place elsewhere, she announced to the abbesss of the monastery that it had occurred. She added that the king who was elected on that day would be killed by his own successor. The outcome confirmed this.[4]

4. Another time, when an evil-doer was threatening our monastery, a danger, which seemed inevitable, was imminent. After she had prayed, she predicted to the abbess that by the grace of God all danger would come to nothing. An official of the court then arrived, who declared that the danger had been averted by a judicial decision—exactly what she had secretly come to understand by divine revelation. This led the abbess and others who knew of this favor to rejoice in the Lord and give him thanks.

5. There was also a certain person who was exhausted by lengthy trials. She was advised in a dream to entrust herself to [Gertrud's] prayers. When she had done this faithfully, she was filled with joy at her immediate release through her merits and prayers of intercession.

6. I also thought the following incident worth mentioning. A certain person who was about to receive communion was obsessed at mass by many thoughts arising from an incident which had taken place several days earlier. Their pressure was such that she was almost inclined to give her consent to their enjoyment. She was extremely disturbed by this, for she did not dare approach with such thoughts on her mind. At length, believing herself divinely inspired, she surreptitiously took a worthless scrap of cloth cut from the covering of the feet of God's chosen one, which she had seen her throw away. With confidence she placed it on her heart

[4]Adolph of Nassau, who succeeded Rudolph, was elected on 1 May 1292. He was deposed and murdered on 2 July 1298 by Albert of Hapsburg.

and begged the Lord, by the love that had led him to choose so graciously the heart of [Gertrud] his beloved, purified of all human affection, to be his alone, to inhabit and to flood with spiritual gifts, and by her merits, that he would condescend mercifully to free her from her temptation. A miracle, truly deserving everyone's acceptance and respect! As soon as she held that scrap of cloth, with the devotion I have described, pressed against her heart, the physical, human temptation was so completely taken from her that she was never troubled by another like it.

7. Let no one think it improper to give credence to this, since the Lord himself says in the gospel, 'Anyone who believes in me will himself do the works that I do, and even greater than these will he do.'[5] The Lord who once condescended to heal the woman with an issue of blood by a touch of the fringe of his garment,[6] could equally, when it so pleased his loving-kindness, draw from the danger of temptation, through the merits of this woman whom he had chosen, a soul for love of which he had condescended to die.[7]

Let this be sufficient evidence from the first witness, although far more could be added.

[5]Jn 14:12
[6]Lk 8:44.
[7]Prayer for the commendation of a departed soul.

CHAPTER THREE

THE SECOND WITNESS

1. A second witness that establishes the truth, is the sober and consistent account given by various people. They declare unanimously that whatever they learned about her through divine revelation, whether they were praying for the correction of their weaknesses or for the increase of their strengths, was always such that she appeared as one specially chosen and exceptionally privileged with superior graces.

As an example, well-established as she was on a solid foundation of humility, she considered herself utterly unworthy of all God's gifts. Sometimes she asked others, whom she considered to be her superiors in grace, for the Lord's testimony upon certain gifts of grace she had received. When they sought this, they were often given reassurance by God's loving-kindness, and they would truthfully assert that the Lord had raised her to a high level, on the basis not only of those gifts of which they had learned from her, but also of far greater gifts of grace besides.

2. Someone with much experience in divine revelation came from a distance to the convent, drawn by the fragrance of its good reputation. As she knew no one there, she expressed in prayer her desire to win from God the promise that he would bring her into contact with someone from whom, with God's help, she could gain spiritual profit. The Lord gave her this reply: 'I

want you to know that the one who first sits beside you, is truly most faithful beyond all others, and truly chosen.' After he had spoken, by an extraordinary chance [Gertrud] was the first to sit beside her; but, wishing out of humility to remain hidden, she kept almost entirely to herself. The visitor thought she had been deceived and put her case before the Lord with downcast heart and cries of lamentation, but she was assured that [Gertrud] really was the one whom the Lord had declared to be most faithful to him. Later, when she heard the words of Dame M[echtild] the chantress of blessed memory,[1] she was highly pleased, as if they had been permeated by the sweetness of the Holy Spirit. She sought from the Lord how it could be that when he praised Gertrud above all others he had not mentioned the other saintly woman. The Lord replied: 'Great are the deeds I perform in the one; but much greater are those I perform in the other, and I shall yet perform in her the greatest of all.'

3. When another person was praying for her, and pondering on the Lord's inestimably delightful love for her, she said to the Lord in great astonishment: 'God, you who are Love, what do you see in her that you make so much of her in yourself, and gently bring your Heart close to her?'[2] The Lord replied, 'My unprompted loving-kindness compels me. By a special gift it has formed and conserved in her soul five things in which I take great pleasure: true purity, from the ceaseless in-pouring of my grace; true humility, from the greatness of my numerous gifts, since the more I work great things in her, the more does she abase herself to the depths of humility, from knowledge of her own weakness; true kindness, which leads her to desire the salvation of all people, with my praise in mind; true fidelity, in that she imparts wholeheartedly, for the salvation of all the world, all the good things that she receives, always with my praise in mind; and true love, which causes her to love me ardently with all her heart, with all

---

[1]This is the way in which the redactor refers throughout to Mechtild of Hackeborn, Gertrud's novice-mistress and spiritual confidante, whose visionary experiences Gertrud wrote down as the *Liber specialis* (or *spiritualis*) *gratiae*. See Introduction, p. 22.

[2]Jb 7:17.

her soul, and with all her strength, and her neighbor as herself,[3] for my sake.'

Then the Lord revealed a splendid necklace lying on his chest, intricately worked with miraculous skill, having three points like a cloverleaf, and said: 'I shall wear this continually in honor of my bride. Its three points will make three things dazzlingly clear to the company of heaven. First, it blazens abroad that she is close to me, for there is no one living on earth who is closer to me than she, by her purity of intention and her good will. Secondly, it shows with burning clarity that there is now no soul on earth toward which I am drawn with as great delight as I am toward her. Thirdly, it makes crystal clear that no one on earth is more faithful to me than she is, in lovingly reflecting back, with my praise and glory in mind, all the gifts conferred on her.' And the Lord added, 'There is nowhere on earth where you can find me more lovingly than in the sacrament of the altar, and consequently in the Heart and soul of this woman who loves me, to whom I miraculously direct all the delight of my divine Heart.'

4. Again, someone else to whose prayers [Gertrud] had devoutly entrusted herself, prayed for her and received this answer: 'I am wholly hers; for I have given myself up to her embraces with complete delight. The love of my godhead has united her insep-arably to me, just as fire makes electrum[4] from gold and silver compounded.' [This woman] said, 'How then do you treat her, most loving God?' He replied, 'The beatings of her heart are un-ceasingly mingled with the beatings of my love, and in this lies my delight, which is beyond all human reckoning. But I am holding back the full force of my own heart-beats until the hour of her death; then she will experience in them three powerful effects: she will know, first, the glory with which God the Father will sum-mon her; secondly, the joy with which I will receive her; thirdly, the love with which the Holy Spirit will unite her to me.'

5. Again, on another occasion someone who was praying for her received this reply: 'She is my dove which has no gall, for she

---

[3]Lk 10:27; see RB 4.1–2.

[4]Electrum was an amber-colored alloy made from gold and silver.

loathes all sin from her heart as if it were gall. She is a lily that I love to hold, for my greatest delight is to take pleasure in a chaste and pure soul. She is my perfumed rose, patient and thankful in times of trouble. She is a full-blown flower in whom my eyes find delight, for she possesses desire and earnest love for virtue and for complete perfection. For all the citizens of heaven she is a bell chiming sweetly on my crown,[5] from which all her sufferings hang like tiny golden spangles.'

6. Again, before Lent, when she was reading aloud the passage set for the community and was reciting with special care, among other things, that we must love the Lord with all our heart, all our soul, and all our strength,[6] one nun, stung by her words, said to the Lord: 'Ah, Lord God, how greatly you are loved by that woman, who teaches with such convincing words that we must love you!' The Lord replied to her: 'From her childhood I have borne and carried her in my embrace, keeping her unspotted for myself, until the moment when she joined herself to me with her whole will; and then in turn I gave myself completely, with all the strength that is mine as God, to her embrace. For this reason her heart's burning love for me ceaselessly caused my inmost being to melt into her, so much so that, as fat melts in the fire, so the sweetness of my divine Heart, melted by the heat of her heart, is distilled continuously into her soul.' And the Lord added, 'My soul takes such great pleasure in her that again and again, when I have been hurt by others, I find pleasant repose upon her, by sending her some physical or spiritual trial. She, in union with my passion, accepts these with such great patience and humility that I am immediately reconciled by her love and have mercy on countless men and women.'

7. Again, when someone was praying for the corrections of [Gertrud's] failings at her own request, she received this answer: 'What seem to my chosen one to be failings in herself are, on the contrary, great sources of strength for her soul. Human frailty would hardly be able to keep the grace which I bring about in her

[5]Ex 28:33–5.
[6]RB 4.1–2.

from the chill wind of vanity, if it were not hidden beneath apparent failings. Just as a field well mulched with manure produces a richer yield, so she, from recognition of her own failings, produce more luscious fruits of grace.' And the Lord added: 'I myself have given her a gift for every one of her failings that corrects them in my eyes. When with the passage of time I have completely transformed them into virtues, then her soul will radiate like a brilliant light.'

Let this evidence be sufficient from the second witness; more will be added at appropriate places.

CHAPTER FOUR

THE THIRD WITNESS

1. Thirdly, an even clearer witness is her own life. She demonstrated for everyone to see, both by what she said and by what she did, how thoroughly she was seeking God's glory and not her own. Not only was she seeking it, but she tracked it down so passionately that in its cause she discounted not only her own honor but even her life and, in a sense, her very soul. And so we should rightly give credence to this witness, in view of the Lord's words in Saint John's gospel: 'One who seeks the glory of him who sent him is truthful, and there is no unrighteousness in him'.[1] O truly fortunate soul, whose life on earth openly reveals that she was in accord with such testimony of evangelical truth! This text from the book of wisdom can truly be applied to her: 'The just man has the confidence of a lion'.[2] In her love for divine praise she worked for justice and truth in all things with such consistency that she completely discounted whatever trouble it entailed, just as long as she was increasing the glory of her Lord.

2. She also devoted a good deal of effort to collecting and writing down everything which she thought might sometime be of use to anyone. She did this purely with God's praise in mind; she

[1]Jn 7:18.
[2]Pr 28:1.

never hoped for anyone's thanks for this, but wished only for the salvation of souls. Consequently she was quick to share what she had written, especially with those in whom she hoped for more success. Also, where she knew there was a special shortage of the sacred books, she willingly did what she could to get hold of the necessary copies, so as to win everyone for Christ. To interrupt the peace and quiet of her sleep, to postpone her meals,[3] to do without anything which concerned the comfort of her own body, these things she considered a joy rather than a trouble. Not satisfied with this, she would also time and again interrupt her enjoyment of contemplation when necessity compelled her to go to the assistance of someone in temptation or to console the afflicted or in charity to help someone. As iron placed in fire immediately becomes all fire, so she, enkindled by the love of God, became all love, desiring the salvation of the world.

3. The conversations she held with the Lord of majesty were so substantial that we knew of no one who matched her in our generation; yet their effect was always to lead her to greater humility. She used to say that as long as she kept all that she had received from God's overflowing goodness to herself, and enjoyed it in isolation, unworthy of the grace and ungrateful for it, it all seemed to her to be lying hidden in dung, because of her worthlessness. But when she had communicated it to someone else, then she thought of it as a precious stone in a gold setting, for she considered everyone to be worthier than herself. She reckoned that everyone else, because of their spotless and worthy lives, could give God greater praise by a single thought than she could accomplish, because of her unworthy life and carelessness, by the full exertion of her body. This alone compelled her to expose anything God bestowed on her to all and sundry, because she judged herself so completely unworthy of all God's gifts that she could not possibly believe that they had been given her for herself alone, but rather for the salvation of others.

---

[3]According to the Benedictine Rule, meals are to be taken later in the day during penitential seasons.

CHAPTER FIVE

ON THE SIGNS AND THE ADORNMENT
OF AN INTELLECTUAL HEAVEN

1. In accordance with what was said above, that every statement should depend on the assertion of two or three witnesses, when the witnesses are so truthful and deserving there is no way in which their truth can be rejected. The incredulous sceptic should rather be overcome with embarrassment because, if he has not deserved to receive similar [graces] himself, he is neglecting to appropriate for himself, by rejoicing with her, those God's generosity has condescended to perform through his chosen one.[1] It seems completely wrong not to acknowledge that this woman is one of his chosen, one of those saints whom Saint Bernard describes in his Sermon on the Song of Songs, when he writes:[2]

> I consider a blessed soul to be not only heavenly because of
> its origin, but also that it can itself properly be called a heaven by

[1]Compare Eckhart, 'A Sermon for St Dominic's Day': 'if you love blessedness in the angels as in yourself, and if you love blessedness in our Lady as in yourself, you will enjoy the same blessedness, in the true sense of the word, as they themselves enjoy. It will be yours just as much as theirs.' (*Meister Eckhart: Selected Treatises and Sermons*, trans. by James M. Clark and John V. Skinner (London, 1958) p. 61.

[2]SC 27:8–10, adapted.

analogy, as its way of life is in heaven.[3] Thus Wisdom says: 'The soul of the just is the throne of wisdom'[4] and 'Heaven is my throne'.[5] Because the writer knows God is a spirit, he does not hesitate to attribute to him a spiritual throne. What especially strengthens me in this belief is the promise, 'We shall come to him', to the holy man, 'and make our home with him'.[6] I think the prophet was speaking of the same thing when he said: 'But you inhabit the holy place, the praise of Israel'.[7] And Saint Paul clearly says that Christ lives in our hearts through faith.[8] From afar do I look with longing on those blessed ones of whom it is said: 'I will dwell in them and walk among them'.[9] How great the breadth of that soul, how great the privilege of its merits, that it possesses in itself the divine presence—that it is found worthy to receive it, and capable of containing it—that its dimensions are enlarged as a place for the divine action! It has grown into a temple holy to the Lord; it has grown, I mean, as measured by love, the unit of measurement for the soul.

A holy soul is a heaven, with understanding as its sun, faith as its moon, and the virtues as its stars. It is even more true to say that its sun is justice or the zeal of ardent love, and its moon is chastity. Nor is it surprising if the Lord Jesus gladly dwells in this heaven. Unlike the other, when he had only to speak, and it came into being, [this heaven] he fought to win, and died to redeem. And so after his labor when he possessed his desire, he said: 'This is my rest for ever; here shall I dwell' and so forth.[10]

2. In order to demonstrate to the best of my ability that she was, as I said earlier, one of those blessed souls whom God (according to Saint Bernard) has chosen as his dwelling in preference to a physical heaven, in her praise I shall set out what I was able to discover

---

[3]Ph 3:20.

[4]Pr 12:23 (LXX); see also Gregory the Great, Homily 38 (ET by D. Hurst, Forty Gospel Homilies, CS 123: 339–356).

[5]Is 66:1.

[6]Jn 14:23.

[7]Ps 21:4 / 22:3.

[8]Eph 3:17.

[9]2 Co 6:16.

[10]Ps 131:14 / 132:14.

about her during the course of many years spent in close spiritual contact with her. Saint Bernard, who has been mentioned often, says that the intellectual heaven—that is, a blessed soul which God condescends to inhabit—ought to have the beauty of the virtues as its adornments of sun, moon and stars. I shall therefore briefly set out here, as far as I can, what special rays of the virtues emanated from her, so that there can be no doubt that the Lord of virtues had his home in her inmost being, whom he had so miraculously made beautiful outwardly, with the loveliness of glittering stars.

CHAPTER SIX

THE CONSTANCY OF THE SUN

1. Now justice, or the zeal of ardent love, which Saint Bernard in the passage quoted earlier is seen to symbolize by the word 'sun', shone from her so surpassingly that, if the occasion had demanded it, she would gladly have exposed herself in its defence in the midst of a thousand battle-lines. Nor did she have any friends so dear that she would have helped them by a single word to act in a way that violated the straight and narrow path of justice, even against her own deadly enemy, if she had one. She would rather have agreed to the injury of her own mother, if a just cause demanded it, than agree to an act of injustice against any enemy, however troublesome to her.

Whenever an opportunity occurred to offer suggestions and advice to people, to encourage them, she would completely disguise her modesty, though this virtue shone quite brightly among her other virtues, and she would put aside timidity as human and out-of-place. She would place her trust in him to whose service she longed to deliver up the whole world by the weapons of faith. She would dip her pen, her powers of expression, in the blood of her heart and choose her words with devout love born of loving-kindness, and grace born of wisdom. Scarcely anyone could be so stubborn and perverse, at least no one having any spark of loving-kindness, as not to be softened by her words, at least to the extent of desiring correction.

If she considered that some had been moved to remorse by the impelling force of her counsels, she leaned toward them with so great a feeling of kindly compassion, and embraced them with such gentle arms of charity, that with melting heart she strove to share herself completely with them, to console them. She did this, I mean, not so much by a show of words as by a devout profusion of prayers and aspirations to God on their behalf.

She was always wary of words, in case she might draw someone into a friendship with herself which might result in her becoming separated, even a little, from God. She turned away from all human friendship which, as far as she could tell, did not have its basis in God, as if it were a mortal danger. She could not listen without great anguish of heart even to a single friendly word from people who behaved toward her in a merely human way. She could not accept any service from them, however essential to her, much preferring to do without any human service or help than to agree to anyone's heart being disproportionately concerned with her.

CHAPTER SEVEN

HER PASSION FOR THE
SALVATION OF SOULS

1. Her words and deeds provide the clearest evidence of the way
in which a passion for souls and an enthusiasm for the religious
life fired her mind. If ever she noticed some failing in one of her
neighbors, she longed to set it right; if she did not see this longing
have any effect, it weighed on her soul so heavily that she was
quite inconsolable until by prayers to the Lord and also by words
of exhortation, made either personally or through intermediaries
whom she was able to invoke, she had won some improvement at
least. But at times it happened, as is the way with human beings,
that someone would say, in the hope of comforting her, that she
should not concern herself with one who refused to amend, as
such a one would have to pay the penalty himself. She dashed this
argument aside with such great sorrow that it seemed as if a sword
were piercing her inmost being. She used to say that she would
rather choose to die than be comforted for someone's failing by
such an argument, because one ought to make the attempt now,
as an eternal penalty would follow death.

For the same reason, if she found anything useful in holy
Scripture which seemed hard for the less intelligent to understand,
she would alter the Latin and rewrite it in a more straightfor-
ward style, so that it would be more useful to those who read it.
She spent her whole life in this way, from early morning until

night, sometimes in summarizing lengthy passages, sometimes in commenting on difficulties in her desire to promote God's praise and her neighbor's salvation.

2. Bede beautifully describes the greatness of this virtue when he writes: 'What way of spending one's life can be more exalted in grace and more welcome to God than that which devotes itself to turning others toward the grace of their Creator by daily exertion, and ever to increasing the joy of our heavenly home by the constant winning of faithful souls?'[1]

Bernard [says]: 'True and pure contemplation possesses this characteristic, that it sometimes fills the mind which it has set ablaze with divine fire with so great a longing to win for God those who would love him in the same way, that it gladly interrupts the repose of contemplation for passionate preaching. When its prayers have been granted, the more the soul is mindful of having interrupted [its contemplation] to good effect, the more ardently it returns to it'.[2] For if, as Gregory testifies, God praises no sacrifice as much as a passion for souls,[3] it is no wonder that the Lord Jesus willingly and generously inhabits this living altar where the sweet odor of his favorite sacrifice rises up to him so often.

3. Once the Lord Jesus, fairest of the children of earth,[4] appeared to her standing and, as it were, with an enormous house on his royal and delicate shoulders. It seemed to be resting on him, but about to fall. The Lord said to her: 'See how hard I labor to bear up my house which I love, that is, the religious life. Throughout almost the whole world it threatens to collapse at any moment because there are so very few in the whole world who are willing to labor faithfully to defend it, or advance it, or even to maintain it. Therefore, my beloved, cast your gaze on me and have pity on my exhaustion.' And the Lord added: 'All those who work for the

---

[1]Bede, Homily on the Vigil of St John the Baptist, CCCM SL 122 (Turnholt, 1955), Homelia II, 19, 290–95. [English translation in Bede: *Homilies on the Gospels* II (CS 111: 188–200)]

[2]SC 57:9.

[3]PL 76:932. See also PL 79:593.

[4]Ps 44:3 / 45:2.

religious life by word or deed lighten in their measure the weight of my burden, as though props have been placed beneath it, and bear it up with me.'

These words stirred the depths of her being, and she was roused the more passionately to pity for the Lord God her lover; she began to strain every nerve in her efforts to work for the religious life, sometimes overtaxing her strength in the strict observance of the Rule,[5] so as to be a good example. Indeed, when she had faithfully adhered for some time to this practice, the kindly Lord could no longer bear the sight of his beloved's hard labor. He wanted to draw her to the repose of a more pleasing contemplation (of which, however, she had not been in the least deprived by the kind of practice I described earlier). Through many who were close to her, he informed her that she was now to rest from this sort of work, and from then on was to place herself wholeheartedly at the disposal of himself, her lover, alone. Aiming high, she devoted herself completely with prompt and eager readiness to the repose of contemplation, concentrating with pleasing alacrity on the one and only intimate friend of her intimate thoughts, who in his turn, she realized, was concentrating exclusively on her by pouring into her his effective grace.

4. Here I would like to add a passage written by a certain person devoted to God. She wrote down what follows as if she had received it from a divine revelation:

> O consecrated bride of Christ, enter into the joy of your Lord,[6] for the divine heart is moved toward you with inestimable sweetness for the faithfulness which led you to toil at so many tasks in defence of the truth, according to his dearest wish, which is also yours. He wishes you to rest in the shade[7] of his most tranquil consolation. For just as a well-rooted tree which has been planted near water to keep it moist bears a more abundant crop, so with the cooperation of God's grace do you bear for your beloved the most delicious fruit from every one of your thoughts, words and deeds. You can never dry up in the

[5]*in rigore Ordinis*
[6]Mt 25:21.
[7]Sg 2:3.

heat of persecution, for again and again you are watered by swelling streams of God's grace. Because in all that you do, you long for God's praise alone and not your own, you bear fruit a hundredfold for your Beloved from all that you would like to accomplish, or would prompt others to do if you could. And moreover the Lord Jesus himself makes up to God the Father on your behalf every failing, in yourself or in others, for which you mourn. It is his plan to reward you for each and every [deed] just as if you had brought them to complete perfection. All the company of heaven, sharing your joy in this, rejoices marvellously and joins together in praise, giving thanks to the Lord on your behalf.

CHAPTER EIGHT

HER COMPASSIONATE LOVE

1. Together with the zeal for justice mentioned earlier, she radiated such a strong feeling of compassionate love that, if she saw someone distressed for good reason, or came to know of someone, even someone far away, who was in trouble, she would immediately do everything in her power either to lessen their distress by speaking to them, or to put new life into them by writing to them. And she used to concentrate on this with such intensity that, like a sick man with a high fever who hopes from one day to the next for release or relief, from one hour to the next she hoped with all her heart that the Lord was consoling those whom she knew to be in trouble.

It was not only toward people but toward every creature that she experienced so strong a feeling of loving-kindness; if she saw any creature, bird or animal, suffering distress from hunger or thirst or cold, from the depths of her loving heart she immediately felt compassion for her Lord's handiwork. She strained every nerve to offer up with devotion, to his eternal praise, the distress of a creature without reason, in union with that dignity which in him fully perfects and ennobles every creature, wishing that the Lord would take pity on his own creation, and condescend to relieve its needs.

CHAPTER NINE

HER WONDERFUL CHASTITY

1. Chastity too, which Saint Bernard set in the heaven of sanctity as its moon, shone brightly in her. She used to say, with complete conviction, that in all her life she had never looked at a man's face with such interest as to know anything about its appearance. And likewise all who knew her could say with her that, however holy the man, however intimately and lengthily she had to speak to him, she parted from him without having looked at him even once. And it can be said not only of her sense of sight, but also of her speech, hearing and her other senses, that the beauty of her wonderful chastity shone so brightly in her that her close friends used sometimes to say jokingly that she ought rightly to be put on the altar among the relics, because of the purity of her heart!

This is not surprising, since it was her habit to take a delight in holy Scripture beyond that of anyone I know, and consequently she also took a delight in God, and this is what chiefly preserves chastity. So Gregory says: 'When one has tasted the spirit, all flesh is distasteful',[1] and Jerome: 'Love the scriptures, and you will not love the vices of the flesh'.[2] But if other evidence were lacking, the clearest indication of chastity shines brightly in this single fact, that

---

[1] Gregory, *Moralia in Job*, 36: also quoted in Bk I, 11:5.
[2] Jerome, *Ep* 125 (PL 22:1078)

she concentrated on the meditative reading of Scripture.[3] Even if she occasionally found something in the scriptures, as sometimes happens, which could in any degree introduce a suggestion of something carnal, guided by her virginal sense of modesty she would, as it were, stealthily omit it and pass it by. Or if she could not do this, she would pretend not to notice it, reading it quickly as if she did not understand it at all—although she was not able to hide the rosy beauty of gracious modesty on her cheeks. But if it happened that the less comprehending asked her questions about such passages she would refuse to answer, claiming ignorance with great modesty. She thought she would hardly find a sword wound to her body more painful than listening to such talk. If, however, it were ever essential to speak of such things for the salvation of souls, she would say what she considered necessary without any hesitation, as if she had no distaste for it at all.

2. Once, when she had confided in an older man of proven experience on the subject of her intimacy [with God], he gave the following testimony, after pondering the purity of her heart: that he had never known anyone as much a stranger to carnal emotion as she was. Therefore (I shall not quote all of it) as he had made careful observation of this single gift of God in her, it was no surprise to him if God had revealed his secrets to her rather than to others, since he says himself in the gospel: 'Blessed are the pure in heart, for they shall see God'.[4] Augustine says: 'God is not seen by the eyes of the body but by the heart, and just as the sunlight can only be seen by eyes cleansed of any impurity, so God can only be seen through purity of heart, a heart which conscience does not accuse of sin but which is the holy temple of God'.[5]

3. As evidence of the virtue we have been discussing I should like to add here what was observed by a certain trustworthy person. When she besought the Lord to condescend to charge her with some message for this woman he had chosen, the one whom we are praising in this book, the Lord replied: 'Say to her from me,

[3]*lectio*, a characteristically monastic expression.
[4]Mt 5:8.
[5]Augustine, *Ep* 147 (PL 33:596).

"Lovely and beautiful" '. When she did not understand and made the same request of the Lord a second and a third time, she received exactly the same reply. Then, quite astonished, she said: 'Explain to me, most loving Lord, the meaning of these words'. The Lord said to her: 'Tell her that the beauty of her inner loveliness pleases me, for the great splendor of my purity and unchanging divinity completely hallows her soul with a beauty beyond comprehension; that the unique beauty of her virtues pleases me, for the joyous verdancy of my deified human nature comes into flower in all that she does with a natural vigor that can never wither'.

CHAPTER TEN

HER GIFT OF TRUST FOR
WHICH SHE WAS FAMOUS

1. How extraordinarily there shone in her, not the virtue but rather the gift of trust, can be proved by extraordinary evidence. She possessed so clear and untroubled a conscience at all times that no trials, no losses, no obstacles, not even her own failings could cast a cloud over it or prevent her from possessing a sure trust in God's kindly mercy. It could not even depress her if the Lord occasionally withdrew his customary grace. It was all the same to her whether she possessed his grace or not; the only difference being that hope gave her strength in occasional times of difficulty, since she knew with complete certainty that all things, without or within, were working together for good.[1] And so, just as one awaits with hope a messenger who brings news that has been long desired, so she would await with joy a richer consolation from God, for which she trusted that the trouble that came before was preparing her.

She never seemed so oppressed or demoralized by her own weakness as not to be raised up by the presence of divine grace to receive whatever gifts of God were most ready for her. When she seemed to herself as dark as a dead coal she would suddenly take on new life with the help of God's grace; when she struggled to

[1]Rm 8:28.

rise up to the Lord by concentration, she would soon receive the likeness of God in herself as if in this very act of returning. Like someone who steps out of darkness into sunlight and is instantly flooded with light, so she felt herself to be flooded with the light of the splendor of the divine presence. She also sensed that she had received all the lovely clothes and ornaments which befit a queen surrounded with variety[2] who stands before the immortal King of the ages, thus made worthy and fit for intimate union with God.

2. She had nevertheless decided that it was right for her—spattered as she was with the stains which are an unavoidable part of human existence—to run frequently to the feet of the Lord Jesus and be washed. But, as we said earlier, when she was aware of a more generous influx of divine mercy, she then gave her willing consent to God's good pleasure in all things and gave herself up as an instrument to display all the workings of love in her and with her, to such an extent that she did not hesitate to play with the Lord God of all the world as his equal.

3. Again, from the trust we mentioned above she possessed such grace concerning the reception of communion, that reading in Scripture or hearing from anyone about the danger run by those who receive communion unworthily[3] could not prevent her from always receiving communion gladly, with a firm hope in the Lord's loving-kindness. She considered her own efforts so feeble and virtually null that she never failed to receive communion even if she had neglected the prayers or other exercises with which people usually prepare themselves. She judged that all human effort, compared to this supremely excellent free gift, is like tiny drops compared to the vast expanse of the ocean. And although she could settle on no way of preparing worthily for communion, nonetheless she placed her trust in the unchanging nature of divine generosity as better than any preparation, and did her utmost to receive the sacrament with a pure heart and devoted love.

[2] Ps 44(45): 10,15.
[3] 1 Co 11:27–29.

She also used to attribute every blessing of spiritual grace which she received to trust alone. She considered the gift to be the more freely given in that she recognized that she had truly received, for free and without any merit on her part, that noble gift of trust from the Giver of every grace.

4. Because of trust, which has been mentioned again and again, she often longed for death—only, however, in union with the divine will—so that hour by hour it was the same to her whether she lived or died.[4] She hoped to reap the reward of blessedness through death, and through life the increase of God's praise. Once when she was walking along it so happened that she slipped at the top of some steps. At once, feeling a wonderful sense of exultation in spirit, she said to the Lord: 'It would be well for me, my dear Lord, if this fall should suddenly become the occasion of my coming to you'. When we asked in astonishment if she were not afraid to die without strengthening by the sacraments of the Church, she replied: 'I do indeed long with all my heart to be strengthened by the most salutary sacraments, but my Lord's will and his pre-ordained plan seem to me the best and most salutary preparation for salvation. Therefore in whatever way he wishes, whether by a sudden death or by one long foreseen, I shall go to him most willingly. For I am certain that by whatever sort of death I go to him or depart, I shall never be without the Lord's mercy, without which I know I cannot by any means be saved, whether my death be long foreseen or sudden'.

5. Similarly, in all that happened she rejoiced, for her mind was always directed steadfastly towards God; in all things a wonderful trust flourished, so much so that one could honestly apply to her the proverb 'One who trusts in God is strong as a lion'.[5] The Lord condescended to provide the following evidence for this virtue. One day when a woman made a certain request of the Lord and

---

[4]Eighth response for the Feast of St Martin.

[5]Pr 28:1. The high status accorded trust (*confidentia*) agrees with Eckhart's view, 'Nothing else that one can do is as fitting as great trust in God. With all those who ever obtained great confidence in Him, He never failed to work great things'. ('Talks of Instruction XIV', in *Selected Treatises and Sermons*, p. 82)

was unable to receive an answer and was astonished at this, the Lord at length gave her this answer: 'I put off an answer concerning what you desire for so long because you, unlike my beloved, have no trust in what my freely-given loving-kindness deigns to work in you. She is well rooted in strong trust, and in everything trusts fully in my loving-kindness. Therefore all that she desires from me, I never deny her'.

CHAPTER ELEVEN

HER HUMILITY AND
MANY OTHER VIRTUES

1. Among her many glowing virtues, shining like twinkling stars, with which the Lord had made her extraordinarily beautiful as a dwelling-place for himself, humility in particular shone out— humility the refuge of all graces and the guardian of all virtues. Persuaded by humility, she considered herself so unworthy of all God's gifts that there was no way she could agree to receive a gift to her own advantage. She thought of herself as a channel through which grace might flow to those whom God had chosen, as the result of some hidden design of God's, since she was herself so completely unworthy and received all God's gifts, the greatest and the least, without the least merit or profit. The only merit she could claim was that she labored to give them away, through what she wrote or said, for the good of her neighbor. This she did with such faithfulness toward God and humility toward herself that again and again she would say to herself, 'Even if after this I am tormented in hell, as I deserve, nonetheless I am glad that the Lord will then gather in others the fruit of his gifts.' She acknowledged no one so worthless, in whom she did not think God's gift more profitably invested than in herself. Nonetheless, she never flinched from being ready for any of God's gifts at any time, and consequently was always ready to dispense them for the advantage of her neighbors, as if they be-

longed less to her than to others who received them through her mediation.

Passing judgment on herself in the light of truth, she saw herself as the most distant among those of whom the prophet says: 'All nations are as nothing in his sight'[1] and earlier, 'Like a speck of dust'[2] and so forth. For just as a speck of dust lying under a twig or some such thing is hidden from the sun's rays by a sliver of shadow, so she by effacing herself did all that she could to deflect the excellence of such noble gifts of God, and to accept those gifts only because he who offered them precedes by his inspiration those whom he calls, and follows with his help[3] those whom he justifies. For herself she retained only the guilt which, so she thought, she revealed in being so ungrateful for, and so unworthy of, such freely-given gifts. But with his glory in mind she could not keep silent about God's loving-kindness toward her. She was careful to bring it to the notice of others with this intention in her heart: 'It is quite wrong for God's goodness toward me not to produce better fruit in others than it can produce in me, an abandoned and utterly worthless creature.'

2. Once when she was walking along, much dejected concerning herself, she said to the Lord, 'I consider that of your great miracles, Lord, this is the most striking: that this earth continues to support me, a most unworthy sinner.' The Lord who raises up all those who humble themselves,[4] was most graciously moved by these words and replied with the greatest kindness: 'The earth willingly offers itself to you to tread upon,[5] while all the grandeur of heaven, with a great and solemn dance of exultation, awaits that most joyful hour when it will deign to bear you up.' Wonderful indeed is the sweetness of God's courtesy, which exalts a soul with greater honor the more the thought of its own worthlessness has plunged it into the depths!

---

[1] Is 40:17.

[2] Is 40:15, 'Ecce insulae quasi pulvis exiguus'.

[3] From the prayer 'Actiones nostras' in the most ancient Thanksgiving after mass.

[4] Lk 18:14.

[5] Gregory, Homily 10.

3. She also despised vainglory so much that, when she was at her devotions or engaged in some good work, if some such thought crossed her mind she willingly yielded to it because she thought, 'If anyone seeing this good work is drawn to emulate it, then your Lord gathers this fruit of praise from your efforts.' She considered that she fulfilled the same function in the Church of God as a scarecrow on a farm: it is good for nothing except at harvest-time, when it is tied to a tree to scare away the birds and so keep the crop safe.

4. Of how much ardor and sweetness of spiritual devotion shone in her, she has left us a most convincing proof in her many writings which are of the greatest value. In addition, he who searches our hearts[6] condescended to provide this evidence of it. When a certain devout man experienced very great devotion in his prayer, he realized the Lord was saying to him, 'Know that the sweetness which you are now enjoying, continually visits that woman whom I have chosen, in whom I have freely chosen to live'.

5. It is clear that she took a wonderful delight in the Lord from the fact that ephemeral pleasures aroused in her an incredible distaste, for as Gregory says, 'When one has tasted the spirit, all flesh is distasteful',[7] and Saint Bernard says that all things are distasteful to one who loves God, as long as he is deprived of him whom he desires.[8] And so on one occasion, wearied by her reflections on the worthlessness of human pleasure, she said to the Lord, 'I can find nothing at all on earth in which I can take pleasure, except for you alone, my most sweet Lord.' Then the Lord returned the compliment by saying, 'In the same way I too find nothing, in heaven or on earth, in which I take pleasure without you, for through love I always link you to my every pleasure. In this way I continually delight in you, in company with all that I delight in; and the more delightful it is for me, the more fruitful it will be for you'.

[6]Ps 7:10.

[7]*Moralia in Job* 36; cf. Bk I, 9, note 1.

[8]See Bernard, Ep 111.

6. As to her constant practice of prayer and vigils, that is clear enough from the fact that there was never a day when she failed to be present at the usual hours of prayer, unless she was sick in bed or, with God's praise in mind, engaged in working for the welfare of her neighbors. And so the Lord, by gladdening her continuously and with great joy, by the consolation of his presence in her prayers advanced her in spiritual practices more than any physical practices could have strengthened her. For she kept the rule of the Order[9] with such great mental pleasure—practices such as attendance at choir, fasts, and communal labor—that she never missed any of them except for a serious reason. Bernard says: 'Ah, when once someone has been inebriated by the taste of love, he straight away meets all toil and pain with a glad smile'.[10]

7. There also shone in her such great nobility of spirit[11] that she could never bear anything which was against her principles for any time at all. In this respect too the Lord praised her to a certain religious who inquired in his prayer what pleased him most in this woman he had chosen. The Lord replied, 'The nobility of her heart'. The man was very surprised at that and, as if undervaluing that quality, he said, 'I thought, Lord, that she had already achieved greater knowledge and ardent love as well, with the help of your grace'. The Lord replied: 'What you thought is true, too; but she has done so by means of the gift of nobility, which is such a blessing that through it she reaches highest perfection by the direct route. For hour by hour she is found fit for my gifts, as she never allows anything to find a place in her heart which could be an obstacle to me'.

8. As a result of this great nobility, she could never bear to keep anything which she did not need but, with permission, again and again she promptly gave it to others; but not indiscriminately, so that she gave more willingly to the needy. Nor did she in this respect put her dearest friends before her worst enemies.

[9]*statuta Ordinis.*
[10]Unidentified.
[11]*libertas spiritus.*

9. If she suddenly felt in her heart that she had to do or say something, she always set about it at once, so as not to be hindered in God's service or in her zeal for contemplation. That this too pleased God is put beyond all doubt by this revelation: Dame M[echtild] the chantress once saw the Lord sitting on his high throne[12] and [Gertrud] walking to and fro before him, often looking at the Lord's face and longing ardently for the emanations from his divine Heart. Greatly astonished by this, she received this answer: 'The life of this woman whom I have chosen is such that, as you see, hour by hour she walks to and fro in my presence as if she desires uninterruptedly, and seeks to know, the good pleasure of my Heart. Hence, when she discovers what is my will in any matter, she sets out at once to accomplish it with all her might, and at once comes back to discover what else is my good pleasure, and faithfully to pursue that too. In this way her whole life yields praise and glory to me'. Then Dame M[echtild] said, 'My Lord, if her life is like this, why then is she able to judge rather severely on occasions the aberrations and failures of others?' The Lord kindly replied, 'Surely because she herself does not allow any blemish to find a place in her heart, and she cannot bear with equanimity the failures of others'.

10. In clothing and things for her use she always required that they should be necessary and useful rather than that they should satisfy her whims or be a source of pleasure. Whatever her things were like, she was fond of them if they helped her to worship God: the book she read very often, the tablet on which she wrote more frequently, and even the books which others were more willing to read or from which they said they gained much instruction and enlightenment, and other similar objects, were the dearer to her because they seemed, as it were, to render the Lord more praiseworthy service. She made use of all the created things the Lord granted her not for her own benefit but for his, to his eternal praise.

And so she took a wonderful joy in using anything for her own benefit, just as if she had offered it up to the Lord on the

---

[12]Is 6:1.

altar to his honor, or had given it away in almsgiving. Whether she slept, or ate, or received anything else whatsoever that was useful, it was her joy to spend it all for the Lord, seeing him in herself and herself in him, according to the Lord's command, 'Whatever you have done to one of the least of my creatures you have done to me'.[13] She reckoned herself, because of her unworthiness, to be the most worthless and the least of all his creatures, and so whatever she allotted herself she considered that she had allotted to the least of God's creatures.

How great a welcome this found in the divine courtesy God revealed to her in the following way. Once when her work had given her a headache and she was trying to relieve it, with God's praise in mind, by sucking an aromatic drug, the kind Lord kindly and gently bent down to her and made believe that the smell of that drug was refreshing him. Then after a little while he straightened up with sweetened breath and said before all the saints with a proud and eager expression as if he were boasting, 'Look at the present that my bride has just given me!' But she found an infinitely greater joy when she had rendered some similar service to one of her neighbors—just as a miser finds great joy in receiving a hundred marks in return for a penny.

11. She shared all her own possessions so completely with the Lord that whenever she was offered a selection of things from which she could choose—food, clothing, or the like—she would shut her eyes and stretch out her hand to take something. She had in mind that if God had already fixed on something for her, she would by this means receive it, dispensed by him in person. Whatever she then grasped she accepted with immense gratitude, as if the Lord had offered it with his own hands. And from that moment onwards, whether it was the best or the worst, she was perfectly happy with it. As she carried out all that she did with this thought in mind, it was for her a source of marvelous pleasure, so much so that she sometimes thought with compassion of the wretched state of pagans and Jews, because they could not share their choices with God in this way.

[13]Mt 25:40.

12. It is also very clear that the virtue of discretion shone in her to no ordinary degree, most especially from the fact that she enjoyed a wonderfully fluent command, beyond that of others, of the sense and the text of Scripture. Nonetheless, although in a single hour she might give prudent answers on a variety of subjects to the many people who sought her advice so that those who heard her were greatly astonished, with humble discretion she asked that others, far inferior to her, should decide what she herself should do. She concurred so heartily with their advice in all matters that it was unusual for her to be so attached to her own decisions as not to follow more willingly the opinion of others.

13. It might seem unnecessary for us now to add, one by one, the other virtues that blazed in her with such dazzling light—that is, obedience, self-restraint, voluntary poverty, prudence, fortitude, moderation, mercy, concord, constancy, gratitude, the ability to share others' joy, contempt of the world, and very many others—since this virtue—that is, discretion, which is called the mother of all the virtues[14]—possessed her soul as its own. Moreover trust, a virtue mentioned earlier, the foundation of all the virtues which obtains all it desires and particularly anything relevant to the other virtues, splendidly enveloped her. In addition that noble and conscientious guardian of the virtues, humility, (as I wrote above) had put down deep roots in her heart. And holding sway over all these, the queen of all the queenly virtues, love of God and one's neighbor, had firmly established its throne in the depths of her being and in her activities, as is shown with great clarity throughout the entire text of this book.

But for the sake of brevity I forbear to expound what I know of each of her virtues one by one, though to run over the many things that should be recited, things to be extolled beyond what has already been mentioned, would induce not boredom but delight in the mind of the devout reader. Therefore let what has been said suffice to demonstrate conclusively that this woman was indeed one of the heavens, or rather that very heaven, in which the King of kings condescends to dwell on his starry throne.[15]

[14]RB 64:19.

[15]Antiphon for Vespers of the Assumption.

CHAPTER TWELVE

CLEARER TESTIMONIES ABOUT
THE INTELLECTUAL HEAVEN

1. Elsewhere, praising the splendor of the intellectual heavens, Scripture says of the apostles: 'They are the heavens in which you live, O Christ; your thunder peals in their words, your lightning flashes in their miracles, your dew falls in their grace'.[1] Therefore, in the small measure that I can, I shall demonstrate in these three ways a little of how she was in harmony with them.

So great and so efficacious a force was present in her words that it was unusual for anyone not to heed them. Whatever she had in mind, her words always prevailed with considerable ease. Hence the verse of Proverbs could deservedly be applied to her: 'The words of the wise are like goads, and like nails deeply fastened'.[2] But nonetheless human weakness sometimes refuses to listen to the truth offered by the force of an ardent spirit. Once when she had distressed one of her close friends by some rather stern words, [the friend], guided by a sense of loving-kindness, strove by prayer to extract from the Lord that he would temper the fervor of her zeal. This was what the Lord taught her: 'When I was on earth, I had extremely strong and passionate feelings; and I too found any kind of injustice in anything totally repugnant. In this respect

---

[1]From the old sequence 'Coeli enarrant' for the feast *Divisio apostolorum.*
[2]Qo 12:11.

77

she is just like me'. Then she said: 'Lord, it was the wicked who thought your words on earth harsh, but that was different from [Gertrud], whose words sometimes distress even those who seem to be good men and women'. To this the Lord replied: 'In those days the Jews were considered to be the holiest of people, but all the same they were particularly offended by me'.

God condescended no less to cause the dew of his grace to fall by means of her words on those whom he had chosen. There are many people who could testify that they once felt greater pangs of remorse at a single word of hers than at a lengthy sermon by seasoned preachers. Another witness to this are the tears, which cannot lie, of those who came to her at a time when they seemed so rebellious that they could not be subdued. After listening to a few words from her, they were pierced with such great compunction that they promised that they would give way in all that they ought.

2. Many people found this grace not only in her words but also in her prayers. When they had entrusted themselves to her prayers, they were so manifestly released from great troubles of long standing that with a profound sense of wonder they often asked their friends to give thanks to God and to her. Nor would it be right to pass over in silence the fact that some were advised in a dream to confide their troubles to her; having done so, they were most certainly released from them. These facts seem to me not very different from the lightning flashes of miracles, since I regard the easing of souls as no less a cause for gratitude than the easing of bodies. But nonetheless, in order to convey more clearly that this woman possessed true and indubitable evidence that the Lord of hosts dwelt in her, I shall add some things by which that same lightning may be more clearly manifested.

CHAPTER THIRTEEN

SOME ADDITIONAL MIRACLES

1. One year, when the weather during March was so cold and harsh that both human beings and their flocks were threatened with death, she heard some people discussing the fact that there was no hope of any harvest that year because, judging from the phase of the moon, the cold weather would not abate for a long time. One day, in the course of a mass at which she intended to receive communion, she prayed with devotion to the Lord for this intention, and also for many others. When she had finished her prayer she received this answer from the Lord: 'I want you to know with certainty that your prayers for all your intentions have been heard.' She replied, 'Lord, if I am to know this with certainty, and if it is indeed right and proper to give you thanks, give me proof that the harshness of this terrible cold is to be moderated'.

Having said this, she paid no more attention to it, but when mass was over, she came out of the choir and found the whole path wet with the melting snow and ice, which had been frozen solid. As everyone saw that this was happening in defiance of the natural course of the weather, they wondered what could have caused it. And since they did not know that the woman God had chosen had asked for it in her prayers, they were saying that this warm spell would, alas, not continue, for it had not come about in the regular way. But then a lovely period of settled spring weather followed, and continued from then on through the whole season.

2. Also at harvest-time, when it was raining more than was wanted and everyone was afraid that the harvest of grain and other produce would be put at risk by this, they offered prayer after prayer. One day she was praying with the others; she importuned the Lord with such powerful and insistent pressure in her prayers, winning him over, that for her sake he would temper the intemperate weather; which he did. For that very day, although there were plenty of clouds to be seen, the sun shed its splendid rays over all the countryside.

3. In the evening, after supper, when the community was going into the yard to carry out some task, the sun was still shining brightly but at the same time rain-clouds hung low in the sky. She groaned from the bottom of her heart and said to the Lord, in my hearing: 'Lord God of the whole world, I do not wish to compel you, as it were, to yield to my will, totally unworthy as it is; if your unbounded goodness is condescending to restrain this rain because of me and against the proper ordering of your righteousness, please let it rain at once and let your most gentle will be fulfilled'. A miracle! Before she had finished speaking, there was thunder and lightning, and drops of torrential rain began to fall. She was stunned and said to the Lord: 'Most merciful Lord, if it is your will, let your goodness restrain itself until we finish the task to which we are bound by obedience'. At her request the kindly Lord restrained that storm until the community had finished that task to which it was bound. When it was finished, while the community was still standing out of doors, such a violent rainstorm, with flashes of lightning and peals of thunder, immediately began that those who stayed in the yard returned soaked to the skin.

4. In many other cases too, quite often by miraculous intervention and as if without any prayers, sometimes just by a light word, she would obtain divine assistance, as in this case. When she was sitting among some bales of straw and a pencil or needle or some other small thing fell from her hand, something which could not possibly be found in such a large pile of straw, she would say in everyone's hearing, 'Lord, however hard I try, it will do no good looking for that! Please grant that I may find it'. Then without even looking as she stretched out her hand, she immediately grasped it in among

the straw, as if she saw it lying on a completely smooth pavement. This was her common practice in all that she had to do, important or unimportant, to call the beloved Patron[1] of her soul to her side, finding him in all things a source of help both totally reliable and perfectly courteous.

5. Finally, when she was again praying to the Lord because of unseasonable winds and drought, she received this answer: 'The motivation which sometimes prompts me to hear the prayers of those whom I have chosen is unnecessary in our relationship; your will is by my grace so completely united with mine that you cannot will anything unless it is what I will. And so, as it is my intention to constrain the hearts of certain rebels, by this unseasonable weather, to have recourse to me for help by praying for this if for nothing else, in this case I am not answering your prayers. Yet you will receive instead a spiritual gift'. Hearing this, she gave her most willing consent, and from then on always took great joy in the fact that her prayers were not answered when she prayed for intentions other than those in accord with God's will.

Saint Gregory testifies that the mark of the sanctity of the good is not to do miracles but to love their neighbours as themselves; enough was said on this earlier.[2] Let these examples be sufficient to prove that the Lord did indeed choose her for his habitation. There is no lack of peals of thunderous miracles to stop the mouths of those who speak wickedness[3] against God's freely-given generosity, and also to strengthen the trust of the humble, those who hope that all the virtues which they rejoice to find given by God in one of the chosen, may be a source of profit for themselves.

[1]*praesul*, 'patron' or 'protector', also used for 'abbot' or 'bishop' in medieval Latin.

[2]For the general sense, see *Dialogues* I, 12, PL 77: 213.

[3]Ps 62(63):12

CHAPTER FOURTEEN

SPECIAL PRIVILEGES
CONFERRED ON HER BY GOD

1. I must here make certain additions, complementing what has already been written—I have had more difficulty in uncovering them than if they had been sealed beneath a heavy stone—and also other evidence of which I received a truthful account from most trustworthy sources.

2. Many people used quite often to ask her advice on certain doubtful points, and in particular whether they should, for one reason or another, refrain from receiving communion. She would advise those who seemed reasonably fit and ready to approach the Lord's sacrament with confidence, as God is gracious and merciful. Sometimes she almost forced them! On one occasion, however, she began to worry—as is the habit of the sincere and honest mind—that she was taking on herself more than she should by giving such replies. And so running to the clemency of the divine loving-kindness, so familiar to her, and trustingly confiding in him her fear, she was comforted by this answer: 'Do not be afraid, but take comfort. Be strong and confident, for I, the Lord God and your Lover, who by my freely-given love created you and chose you in whom to dwell and take delightful pleasure, I give a definite answer, beyond all doubt, to all who ask me this question with devotion and humility through you. You shall hold this sure

promise from me, that I will never allow anyone whom I judge to be unworthy of the life-giving sacrament of my body and blood to seek out your advice on this. So if I chose to send you for assurance anyone who is weary or oppressed, you shall declare to that person that it is safe to approach me. Because of your grace and love, I will never bar them from my fatherly heart, but I shall open my arms to them, to embrace them in dearest love; nor shall I deny them the delectable kiss of peace'.

3. Hence, when she was praying for someone with more fervor, fearing that person might be hoping to be able to receive more through [Gertrud] than she could gain for herself, the Lord replied very kindly: 'As much as anyone hopes to be able to gain through you, she will certainly receive from me. Moreover, whatever promise you make anyone on my behalf, I shall certainly keep. Even if the person concerned is prevented by human weakness from being aware of the effect, nonetheless I shall carry out in her soul the improvement you promised'.

4. Some days later, remembering the promise the Lord had made and not forgetting her own unworthiness, she asked the Lord how it could possibly come about that he condescended to perform such wonderful miracles through her, totally worthless as she was. The Lord replied: 'Does not the Church's faith rest universally on the promise I once made to Peter alone when I said, "Whatever you shall bind on earth shall be bound also in heaven"[1]? And does not the Church firmly believe that this has come about to the present day through all the ministers of the Church? Therefore why do you not believe with equal faith that I am able and willing to do anything, prompted by love, which I promise you with my divine mouth?' And touching her tongue he said: 'There! I have put my words in your mouth,[2] and I confirm in my truth every single word that you might speak to anyone on my behalf, at the prompting of my Spirit. And if you make a promise to anyone on earth on behalf of my goodness, it will be held in heaven as a promise that has been irrevocably validated'. She said

[1] Mt 16:19.
[2] Jer 1:9.

in answer to this: 'Lord, I would not rejoice if anyone should suffer condemnation as a result of this—if I, under the impulse of the Spirit, told someone that some guilty act could not remain unpunished, or something like that'. The Lord replied: 'Every time that you are impelled by justice or your passion for souls to say such things, I shall surround that person with my loving-kindness, moving her to compunction so that she will not deserve my vengeance'.

Then she asked the Lord: 'Lord, if you speak the truth through my mouth, as your loving-kindness deigns to assert, how is it that my words sometimes have so little effect on people—words I sometimes offer up for the salvation of souls with such a great longing for your glory?' The Lord replied: 'Do not be surprised that your words sometimes labor in vain. I myself, during my earthly life, preached many times in the ardor of my divine Spirit, and nonetheless my words brought about no improvement in some. In my divine plan, all things have their time'.

5. In addition, when she had criticized someone's deficiency, she took refuge in the Lord, praying humbly that he would condescend so to enlighten her understanding with the light of his divine knowledge that in no case would she give anyone an answer other than that pleasing to his divine will. The Lord replied: 'Do not be afraid, my daughter, but have faith that I am conferring a special privilege on you. When anyone asks your advice in humility and faith on any matter whatsoever, in the light of my divine truth you will discern that case and come to the same conclusion as I would in respect to its fundamental nature and that of the person concerned. If I judge someone's case to be quite serious, your answer on my behalf will be quite severe; and again, if I judge someone's case to be less serious, I shall make you answer in gentler terms'.

Then recognizing in the spirit of humility[3] her own unworthiness, she said to the Lord: 'O Ruler of heaven and earth, take back, and keep back, the extravagant profusion of your generosity, for I am dust and ashes,[4] totally unworthy of so great a gift'. The

[3]Dan 3:39; see the Offertory of the Mass.
[4]Gn 18:27.

Lord replied, soothing her kindly: 'Why is it such a great thing for me to grant you to discern the reasons for my enmity when I have allowed you again and again to experience the secrets of my friendship?' And the Lord added: 'Any who are oppressed or sad, who humbly and honestly look for consolation in your words, will never be deprived of their desire. I, God, dwelling in you, at the prompting of the unbounded loving-kindness of my love, long to bring blessings on many people through you. The joy your heart feels at this, it really and truly draws up from the brimming well of my divine Heart'.

6. On another occasion she was praying for those who had been entrusted to her and received this reply from the Lord: 'At one time anyone who grasped the horn of the altar rejoiced at having found peace. Now, because I have chosen you so generously as my dwelling, anyone who confidently entrusts himself to your prayers shall be saved by my grace'.

This receives strong support from the evidence of Dame M[echtild] the chantress of blessed memory; while she was praying for [Gertrud] she was shown her heart in the likeness of a very strong bridge, which seemed fortified on one side by Christ's human nature and on the other by his divine nature, as if they were its parapets. And she understood that the Lord was saying: 'All those who struggle to reach me over this bridge will never be able to fall or wander off the path'; that is, anyone who is receptive of her words and humbly obeys her advice will never wander from the true path.

CHAPTER FIFTEEN

HER BOOK WRITTEN AT
THE LORD'S COMMAND

1. After this, when she had come to realize that it was God's will that all this should come to be known by others through being written down, in her astonishment she turned over in her mind what its utility could be. She knew it was the fixed intention of her heart not to allow this to be made known to others in any way as long as she was alive, and after her death she thought it would result in nothing except disturbing the members of the Church who came to know of it, as they would not be able to gain any profit from it. The Lord replied to these thoughts by saying: 'What do you think is the utility of reading Saint Catherine's account of my visiting her in prison and saying: "Be steadfast, daughter, for I am with you" or of my visiting my beloved John and saying: "Come to me, my beloved", and many other accounts of the experiences of these and others? Is it not that people's devotion grows as a result, and my loving-kindness toward humankind is revealed?' The Lord added: 'The mind of some can be set ablaze with longing for those graces they hear you received; and while they consider this, they will do all they can to amend their own life'.

2. Another time, she was again wondering why the Lord was for so long urging her, through his Spirit, to make public what she had written. She knew that some people are so poor-spirited

that, undervaluing such experiences, they often denigrate them rather than draw any sort of enlightenment from them. The Lord taught her by these words: 'I have so invested my grace in you that I demand a large return for it! So I will that those who possess similar gifts, and through negligence do not realize their true value, should grow in gratitude when they hear about you. They are to achieve a true recognition of their own gifts, and my grace may in this way increase in them. But if any, out of malice, decide to denigrate these things, let their sin be upon them while you remain untouched. The prophet has said on my behalf: "I shall set a stumbling block in their way" '.[1]

These words led her to understand that the Lord often prompts those whom he has chosen to do things which sometimes shock others. However, his chosen are not to refrain from acting out of a hope of keeping peace with the wicked, for the best sort of peace is when good overcomes evil, that is, when someone, not refraining from what perfects God's praise, overcomes the wicked by winning them over with pliancy and good will, for this is the way to enrich one's neighbor.[2] If it does no good, these still do not lose their own reward.[3] Hugh says: 'As those who believe always have something which leads to doubts, while those who do not believe have something that could lead them to belief if they wished, so it is right that believers should receive a reward for their belief and unbelievers punishment for their unbelief'.[4]

[1]Ezk 3:20.
[2]Mt 18:15.
[3]Mk 9:40.
[4]*De Arca morali* 4:3, PL 176:668.

CHAPTER SIXTEEN

FURTHER EVIDENCE OF
THE AUTHENTICITY OF HER
EXPERIENCES CONVEYED BY
THE LORD THROUGH THE
REVELATIONS OF OTHERS

1. Pondering her own worthlessness and unworthiness, since she considered herself totally unworthy of God's great gifts, with which she knew the Lord had faithfully honored her, she came to M[echtild] of blessed memory, who was at that time extremely well-known and respected for the gift of her revelations. Humbly she begged her to ask the Lord's advice on the gifts described above. It was not that she had doubts and wanted to be given reassurance on what she had received; she was longing to be stimulated to greater thanksgiving for such freely-given gifts, and to be reassured in advance, in case her great unworthiness might sometime force her to lapse into doubt. When Dame M[echtild], in accordance with what had been asked of her, had given herself to prayer, asking the Lord's advice, she saw the Lord Jesus, the fresh and tender bridegroom, beautiful beyond thousands of angels, dressed in green garments which seemed to be lined with gold. He was gently embracing with his delicate right hand that woman for whom she was praying, so that her left side, where the heart lies, was as it were pressed against the opening of his wound

of love. She, in return, seemed to be embracing him with her left hand at his back.

In her astonishment blessed M[echtild] longed to know what this vision meant. The Lord said to her: 'You should know that the greenness of my garments, which are lined with gold, signifies that the entire working of my divine nature grows green and flowers from love'. He repeated the phrase, saying: 'It all grows green and flowers in that soul! That you see her heart next to the wound in my side, tells you that I have moulded her heart to me in such a way that she is continuously able to receive, without any intermediary, the influx of my divine nature'.

Then Dame M[echtild] asked: 'Have you, my Lord, given such gifts to this woman you have chosen—that she can safely send on their way, in true knowledge of you, all those who come to her asking for anything at all; that all who seek, through her, the help of true salvation[1] will find it— such gifts as you deigned to promise her in those words which she revealed to me, in seeking their elucidation because of humility?' With great kindness the Lord answered: 'I have indeed invested her with these special privileges, so that whatever anyone can hope to be able to receive through her, that person will certainly obtain; and anyone whom she considers worthy to receive communion, my mercy will never consider unworthy. On the contrary, if she encourages someone to receive communion, I shall look on that person with greater love; and in accordance with my divine insight she will give a considered judgment, as to whether they are more or less serious, on the faults of all those who question her'.

'And as there are three who give evidence in heaven, the Father, the Word and the Holy Spirit,[2] she must always confirm their evidence in three ways: first, if she feels the inner compulsion of the Spirit when talking to someone; secondly, if she sees that the person she is talking to is sorry for the fault, or at least would like to be sorry; thirdly, if she considers that person's will to be virtuous. When she pays careful attention to these three considerations, let her confidently and unhesitatingly answer whatever she thinks, for I shall certainly consider as authorized any pledge she makes

[1]Postcommunion of the mass *de Beata*.
[2]1 Jn 5:7.

anyone, on behalf of my loving-kindness'. And the Lord added: 'Whenever she intends to speak to someone, let her first groan, and through that groan let her draw into herself the exhalation of my divine Heart. Whatever she then says will be absolutely true, for neither she nor those who hear her can possibly be wrong in thinking that the secret of my divine Heart is made known through what she says'. And the Lord added: 'Let her preserve a careful statement of what you say; if after a while she feels the grace she has received growing lukewarm because of her various activities, as often happens, let her not lose faith. I shall certainly keep inviolate in her the gifts of the privileges already described, all the days of her life'.

2. She also asked the Lord whether or not [Gertrud] incurred some guilt by always acting at once if anything came into her mind, and by its being a matter of indifference to her conscience whether she prayed, wrote, read, taught her neighbors, criticized or consoled. The Lord replied: 'I have united my heart with her soul so generously and so inseparably that her spirit is effectively one with mine in all things and above all things. She exists in harmony with my will just as the limbs of her own body exist in harmony with her heart. As someone thinks in the heart, do this, and at once the hand moves harmoniously to carry out the intention; and someone thinks, look at that, and instantly the eyes harmoniously open without delay: so is she often with me as I work with her, so that she is from minute to minute accomplishing what at that time I intend. I have chosen her to dwell in, so that her will, and consequently the operation of her virtuous will, are one with my Heart; she is like my Heart's right hand by which my will is accomplished. Her understanding is like my eye, when she understands what gives me pleasure; the impulse of her spirit is like my tongue, when impelled by the Spirit she says what I intend; her spiritual insight is like my nostrils, for I mercifully give ear to those things to which she is drawn through the loving-kindness of her compassion; her intention is like my feet, when she intends the course which it is right for me to follow. Hence she is right to hurry, following the impulse of my Spirit, so that moving quickly from one task, in conformity with my inspiration, she may be found ready for another. Nor can what remains necessarily

incomplete weigh on her conscience, since in her new task my will is fulfilled'.

3. Another person, expert in knowledge of the spiritual life, while praying and devoutly giving God thanks for the graces he had bestowed on her, was granted so similar a revelation on the gifts of the privileges decribed earlier, and on her union with God, that it was established beyond any shadow of doubt that this had flowed from God, whose testimonies are exceedingly sure.[3] Each of these people had caught with the ears of their understanding the streams of his whispering, like the sigh of a gentle breeze,[4] although the one knew as little of the other's revelation as the inhabitants of Rome can know of what at that moment the inhabitants of Jerusalem are doing.

This woman, at that point in the account of her revelation, added that it had been made known to her that everything that [Gertrud] had received by the gifts of God's graces would be little in comparison with those things with which the Lord still planned to inundate her soul. And she added: 'She has yet to achieve such union with God that her eyes will see only what God deigns to see through them, her mouth will say only what God deigns to say through it, and so on'. How and when the Lord would carry this out is known to him alone and to that woman whose good fortune it is to experience it; but it was not hidden from those who recognized with greater perception the gift of God in her.

4. Another time she asked Dame M[echtild] to pray specially on her behalf, doing her utmost to win for her from the Lord the virtues of gentleness and patience. These she thought she greatly lacked. Dame M[echtild] was praying as she had been asked, and received this answer from the Lord: 'The "gentleness" which I like in her derives its name from "remaining".[5] Because I dwell [in her] it adorns her continually at every moment so that she is like a tender bride who has her bridegroom with her. If she has to go out, she clings to his hand and pulls him, compelling

[3]Ps 92:5 / 93:5.
[4]1 K 19:12.
[5]*mansuetudo*, gentleness, derived from *commanere*, remain, dwell.

him to go out with her. So whenever she sees that it is right to leave the delightful repose of her inner enjoyment to teach her neighbors, let her always first trace the cross of salvation on her breast and with a single word murmur my name, and then let her confidently say in my grace whatever comes to mind. Similarly, the "patience" which I like in her takes its name from "peace" and "knowledge".[6] Let her pursuit of patience be such that she does not lose her heart's peace through adversity; let her always concentrate on knowing why she is suffering patiently— namely, for love, as a sign of true fidelity'.

5. Someone else to whom she was a complete stranger, except that she had entrusted herself to his prayers, received this reply when praying for her: 'I have chosen to dwell in that woman because I am delighted that everything people love in her is my doing; so much so that anyone who did not know her inner, that is, her spiritual qualities, would at least love in her my outer gifts, such as her ability, eloquence, and so on. And thus I banished her from all her relatives so that no one would love her on account of her family connections; consequently I alone am the reason all her friends love her!'

6. Another person asked the Lord at her request why she, who had for so many years an awareness of the divine presence, still seemed to live very imperfectly, but had never committed a fault so serious as to know the Lord to be displeased by her faults. This was the reply: 'The reason I never appear to her angry is that she judges all that I do as entirely equitable and excellent, and she does not allow herself to be greatly disturbed by anything I do. If something happens that is troublesome to her, its burden is always lessened by her knowledge that it has come about through my divine plan; and so, as Saint Bernard says that "one who finds God pleasing cannot be unpleasing to God",[7] I always show myself to her as appeased'.

---

[6]*patientia*, patience, derived from *pax*, peace, and *scientia*, knowledge.

[7]The reference to Bernard was probably originally a marginal gloss, incorporated accidentally into the text. The point of the remark lies in a play on *placere*, 'please', and *placare*, 'appease', two words that are indeed etymologically related.

When [Gertrud] learned that the Lord had of his own clemency given these answers, she was stimulated, as she said, to extreme gratitude. For such generosity she gave the Lord devout thanks, adding among other things: 'How can it be, my most beloved Lover, that your loving-kindness condescends to overlook my many serious evil deeds?—not that your perfect handiwork displeases me, my God, since this is not the result of my virtue but rather of your perfect blessedness'. The Lord enlightened her by means of this analogy: 'When a reader sees that the script of a book is so tiny that he thinks it difficult to read, he picks up a magnifying glass through which the writing looks larger. This is not the doing of the book but of the magnifying glass! In the same way, out of the abundance of my loving-kindness I compensate for any failing that I find in you'.

CHAPTER SEVENTEEN

HER CLOSER INTIMACY WITH GOD

1. At one time the Lord had not visited her for some time. She felt no distress at this, but on one occasion when she had the chance she asked the Lord why this was. The Lord replied: 'Too great a closeness sometimes hinders friends, so that they see one another less clearly. For instance, when someone is united with another, as usually happens with kissing and embracing, the pleasure of seeing one another is impeded for a while'. She understood from these words that sometimes the withdrawal of grace increases merit, as long as a person does not, through the withdrawal of grace, act more sluggishly, even though burdened.

2. While she was turning over in her mind how the Lord was now visiting her with his grace in a different way from before, the Lord added: 'At first I quite often enlightened you by means of replies with which you could make known to others my good pleasure; but now when you pray it is only in your spirit that I make you feel my inspiration, which it would sometimes be very difficult to put into words for the benefit of your mind. I am, as it were, amassing the riches of my grace in your treasury. My intention is that whatever anyone looks for they will find in you, as in a bride who knows all the secrets of her spouse, and from living with him over a long period knows how to carry out his wishes in all that has to be done. It would not be fitting, however, for

her to reveal her spouse's secrets, which are hers thanks to their mutual intimacy'.

3. And so she herself experienced this a little, when she realized that when she prayed for some intention which had been pressingly entrusted to her, she was quite unable to wish to obtain an answer from the Lord, as she had done earlier. It was now quite enough for her when she was aware of the grace of praying for some intention, for she held this impulse to be authentic, as she had before held the divine answer.

Similarly, whenever anyone sought advice or encouragement from her, she instantly felt the grace to answer flooding into her at that moment, with such great confidence that she would dare to endure death fearlessly to assert the truth of her words, although she had never before understood anything about the subject from her reading, from conversation or even from her own thoughts.

When she prayed for some intention on which she received no revelation from the Lord, she took a deep pleasure in the fact that the divine wisdom is unsearchable and so inseparably united with kindly love that the safest thing of all is to entrust all things to it. At such times this pleased her more than if she had been able to fathom all God's profoundest secrets.

BOOK TWO

PROLOGUE

THE NINTH YEAR OF HER FAVORED state had run from February to April[1] when, on the evening of Holy Thursday, she was standing with her sisters waiting for the body of the Lord to be carried to a sick nun. Compelled by the Holy Spirit, she snatched up the tablet hanging at her side. Out of the overflowing abundance of thanksgiving, to his praise, she described with her own hand in these words that follow her sensations when she held intimate converse with her Beloved.

[1]In 1289 (see 'Endorsement and Authorization', p. 29 above).

CHAPTER ONE

HOW THE LORD FIRST VISITED HER AS THE DAYSPRING FROM ON HIGH

MAY THE DEEP OF UNCREATED WISDOM CALL to the deep of wonderful Omnipotence, to praise and exalt such breath-taking Goodness, which guided the overflowing abundance of your mercy down from on high to the valley of my wretchedness![1]

I was twenty-five years old. It was the Monday (a Monday most beneficial for me) before the Feast of the Purification of Mary, the Lord's most chaste mother, which fell on 27 January that year,[2] at the longed-for time after Compline, as dusk began. You, O God, Truth shining brighter than every light yet more inward than every hidden secret,[3] had resolved to temper the thick mist of my darkness. You began gently and easily[4] by calming that storm which, for the past month, you had stirred up in my heart. By that tempest, I believe, you were attempting to pull down the tower[5] of vanity and worldliness into which my pride had grown,

[1] Ps 41(42):8.
[2] AD 1281.
[3] Augustine, *Confessions* 9:1.
[4] Gen 50:21.
[5] Gen 11.

even though I bore—an empty boast—the name and habit of the religious life. All this you did to find a way to show me your salvation.[6]

2. At the hour already mentioned, then, I was standing in the middle of the dormitory. On meeting an elder sister, according to the custom of our Order I bowed my head. As I raised it I saw standing beside me a young man. He was lovely and refined, and looked about sixteen; his appearance was such as my youth would find pleasing. With kindly face and gentle words he said to me, 'Your salvation will come quickly; why are you consumed by sadness? Do you have no counsellor, that sorrow has overwhelmed you?'[7]

While he said this, although I knew I was physically in the place mentioned, it seemed to me that I was in choir, in the corner where I used to make my lukewarm devotions, and it was there that I heard the following words: 'I shall free you and I shall deliver you; do not fear'. At these words I saw a tender, finely-wrought hand holding my right hand as if confirming what had been said with a promise. He added, 'You have licked the dust with my enemies,[8] and you have sucked honey among thorns; return to me at last, and I shall make you drunk with the rushing river of my divine pleasure!'[9]

While he spoke, I looked and saw that between us (to his right and to my left) there was a hedge of such endless length that I could not see where it ended in front or behind me. On its top the hedge seemed to bristle with such a great mass of thorns that I would never be able to cross it to join the young man. While I stood hesitating because of it, both burning with desire and almost fainting, he himself seized me swiftly and effortlessly, lifted me up, and set me beside him. But then I recognised on that hand, from which I had received the promise already mentioned, the glorious gems of those wounds which cancelled the debts[10] of all.

[6]Ps 49:23 / 50:23.
[7]Response for the second Sunday in Advent.
[8]Ps 71:9 / 72:9.
[9]Ps 35(36):9.
[10]Col 2:14.

I praise, adore, bless and offer thanks (as far as I can) to your wise mercy and merciful wisdom. For you, my Creator and Redeemer, were trying in this way to make my stiff neck submit to your mild yoke, by concocting with the utmost gentleness a drink suitable for my sickness. For from that time forward, calmed by a new joy of the spirit, I began to go forth in the delightful perfume of your balm, so that I too thought easy the yoke and light the burden[11] which a little before I had reckoned unbearable.

[11]Mt 11:30.

CHAPTER TWO

ENLIGHTENMENT OF HEART

1. Hail, my salvation and the light of my soul.[1] May all that is encompassed by the path of heaven, the circle of the earth[2] and the deep abyss give you thanks for the extraordinary grace with which you led my soul to experience and ponder the innermost recesses of my heart. These had been of as little concern to me before, if I may say so, as the soles of my feet! But then I became anxiously aware of the many things in my heart which would be offensive to your most chaste purity, and of all the other things so disordered and chaotic that my heart could offer no resting place to you who wished to dwell there.[3] But no more than all my worthlessness did this drive you away, Jesus my most beloved, or prevent your honoring me frequently with your visible presence on those days when I came to the life-giving food of your body and blood. Though I could see you no more clearly than one sees thing at dawn, nonetheless with kindly condescension you induced my soul to exert itself, that it might be united with you more closely.

[1]Ps 26:1 / 27:1.
[2]Est 13:10.
[3]Jn 14:23.

2. I planned to work at achieving this on the Feast of the Annunciation, when you betrothed our human nature to yourself in the Virgin's womb. But you who say 'Here I am!'[4] before you are summoned, anticipated that day by forestalling me, unworthy as I was, in the blessings of sweetness.[5] On the vigil of that feast, because it was a Sunday, chapter took place after Lauds. I cannot find the words to describe how you, the Dayspring from on high,[6] then visited me through the depths of your loving-kindness and sweetness. Giver of gifts,[7] give me this gift: may I henceforward offer on the altar of my heart a sacrifice of joy, that by my supplication I may win for myself and all those whom you have chosen the privilege of enjoying often that sweet union and unifying sweetness, which was quite unknown to me before that hour! For acknowledging the nature of my life before and since, I declare in utter sincerity that it was a grace given freely and undeservedly. From that time forth you endowed me with a clearer light of knowledge of you, in which the sweet love of your loveliness always attracted me more greatly than the harsh punishment I deserved ever castigated me.

I do not remember, however, having ever enjoyed such fulfillment except on the days when you invited me to taste the delights of your royal table. Whether your wise providence ordered this, or my assiduous neglect brought it about, is not clear to me.

[4]RB Prol 18, after Is 58:9 and 70:24.
[5]Ps 20:4 / 21:4.
[6]Lk 1:78.
[7]From the Pentecost sequence 'Veni, Sancte Spiritus'.

CHAPTER THREE

THE PLEASANTNESS OF
THE LORD'S INDWELLING

1. This was how you dealt with me, this was how you aroused my soul on a certain day between Easter and Ascension. I had gone into the courtyard before Prime and was sitting beside the fishpond absorbed by the pleasantness of the place. The crystalline water flowing through, the fresh green trees standing around, the freedom of the birds, especially of the doves, wheeling in flight, all gave me pleasure: but most of all the secret peace of a secluded place of rest. I began to turn over in my mind what I would like to add to this which would make my pleasure in that resting-place seem complete. This was my request: that I might have there a lover—affectionate, able and companionable—to relieve my solitude.

I trust, my God, that it was you—you who produce pleasures beyond price—who had anticipated me and guided the beginning of this meditation; and it was you, too, who drew its conclusion to yourself in such a way. You inspired me with the knowledge that if I poured back like water the flowing streams of your graces with constant and proper thanksgiving, I would grow in a zeal for virtue like the trees and would blossom with a fresh flowering of good works. Moreover, if I looked down on the things of earth and, in free flight like the doves, sought the things of heaven, and if my outer self with its bodily senses were held aloof from hustle and bustle, my mind would be completely at your disposal and my heart would offer you a dwelling-place with all that is pleasant and joyful.

2. Since my mind had been busy all day long with these thoughts, in the evening when I knelt in prayer, about to sleep, there suddenly came into my mind this verse of the gospel: 'If anyone loves me, he will keep my words and my Father will love him, and we will come to him and make our home with him'.[1] Meanwhile my heart of clay realized that you had indeed come and were there present. Oh, how I wish—how many thousand times do I wish—that I could pour over my head all the sea that turned into blood,[2] to flood the cistern of my utter worthlessness in which you, the ultimate manifestation of a worth beyond human thought, chose to live! Or, would that my heart might be given me for an hour, drawn out of my body, to be assayed piece by piece by white-hot coals! Its dross melted away,[3] it might offer, if not a worthy home, at least one not as unworthy of you.

For this was how you, my God, showed yourself to me from that time, sometimes more soothing, sometimes more severe, according to whether I was amending or neglecting my life. Although, to tell the truth, if the most painstaking amendment which I ever, even for a moment, achieved had lasted all my life, it could not by any means have merited even the single most severe appearance which I ever experienced after numerous faults and, alas, grave sins. For your great sweetness made you often pretend to be more concerned than angry with what I had done. It seems to me that you showed greater strength of patience in bearing so calmly such great faults of mine than when in the time of your mortal life you bore with Judas the betrayer.

3. For although I wavered mentally and enjoyed certain dangerous pleasures, when I returned to my heart—after hours and even after days, alas, and after weeks, I fear to my great sorrow—I always found you there. The result is that I could never complain that

[1]Jn 14:23.
[2]Ps 77:44 / 78:44.
[3]Is 1:25.

you withdrew from me for even the blink of an eye from the hour mentioned to the present day, now that nine years have passed. The only exception was on one occasion, eleven days before the Feast of Saint John the Baptist: this happened, so it seems to me, as a result of a worldly conversation on a Thursday, and lasted until the Monday, which was the vigil of the feast,[4] in the course of the mass 'Fear not, Zacharias'. Your gentle humility, and the wonderful goodness of your wonderful divine love, saw me in such a state of abandoned madness that I did not care that I had lost such a treasure. I cannot recall having mourned its loss or having the least wish for its return. I wonder now what madness had taken my mind prisoner, unless it was perhaps your intention to allow me to have personal experience of what Bernard says: 'As we flee you pursue us; we turn our backs and you run to meet us face to face; you plead but are scorned. But no embarrassment or scorn can turn you aside or stop you from acting unwearyingly to draw us to that joy which eye has not seen, not ear heard, and which has not risen into the heart of man'.[5] As I was undeserving in the first place, so you deigned to bestow the joy of your saving presence[6] on me who had done more than simply fail to deserve it, for it is worse to re-lapse than to lapse; and it has continued to this day. For this be praise and thanksgiving to you—that thanksgiving which, going gently forth from uncreated Love and incomprehensible to all created being, flows back to you.

4. For preserving so great a gift I offer you that most excellent prayer[7] which, as your bloody sweat testifies, the pain of strait necessity made strong, the innocence of pure simplicity made devout and the love of white-hot divinity made potent. By the power of that same most perfect prayer, perfect me completely in union with you and draw me to yourself in my heart of hearts. Then whenever it happens that I must devote myself to external works for practical purposes, may I be given to them on loan, as

---

[4]In 1281, the year of Gertrud's conversion, June 23 fell on a Monday.

[5]The source of this quotation has not been identified. The last phrase echoes 1 Co 2:9.

[6]Ps 50:14 / 51:14.

[7]1 Jn 17:1–26, presumably with specific reference to 22–23.

special cases:[8] then when they have been perfectly completed to your praise, may I return at once to you in my heart of hearts, as the general rule, just as the tumultuous rush of water flows back to the depths, when whatever barred the way has been removed.

For the rest, may you often find me concentrating as much on you as you show yourself to be present to me. By this may you lead me to such perfection as ever your justice permitted a soul to achieve, a soul burdened by the weight of flesh and so completely resistant to your mercy. As it breathes its last within your most strait embrace and most potent kiss, may my soul find itself without delay there where you, unbounded and indivisible, live and are glorious in flourishing eternity with the Father and the Holy Spirit, true God throughout unending ages.

[8]*particulariter . . . universaliter.*

CHAPTER FOUR

THE IMPRINTING OF THE
LORD'S MOST HOLY WOUNDS

1. In the early stages of these events, in the winter of the first or second year, I think, I found in a book a little prayer that went as follows:

> Lord Jesus Christ, Son of the living God, grant that I may aspire to you with all my heart, with abundant desire, with thirsting soul. Grant that I may respire in you, who are most sweet and most delightful. Grant that my whole spirit and all my inner being may unceasingly pant after you who are true blessedness. Most merciful Lord, write your wounds[1] in my heart with your precious blood, that I may read in them your suffering and your love alike. Then may the mindfulness of your wounds remain with me unceasingly in the recesses of my heart, that sorrow for your suffering may be aroused in me and the ardor of your love may be kindled in me. Grant also that all creation may grow worthless in my eyes, and that you alone may impart sweetness to my heart.

---

[1]On devotion to the Five Wounds see L. Gougaud OSB, *Devotional and Ascetic Practices in the Middle Ages*, trans. by G.C.Bateman (London, 1927) pp. 80–91, and R.W.Pfaff, *New Liturgical Feasts in Later Medieval England* (Oxford, 1970) pp. 84–91.

2. I was in complete agreement with the sentiments this little prayer expressed, and I was eager to repeat it ardently when you, who never despise the supplications of the humble, came to me ready to offer the fulfilment of that little prayer. A short while later during that same winter, I was sitting in the refectory at supper after Vespers beside a certain person[2] to whom I had, in part, revealed the secrets of my experiences. I add this here for the benefit of the reader, for I often felt the fervor of my devotion increased by such an interchange. Whether it was your Spirit, Lord God, that prompted this or human affection, is not clear to me. I have however heard from someone skilled in such matters that such a secret may be more profitably revealed to someone who is not only a close friend by reason of her faithful goodness but also a superior by reason of the respect due to greater age. But since I know nothing of this, as I said before, I entrust the matter to you who keep most faithful watch over me, whose Spirit, which is sweeter than honey,[3] maintains the whole strength of heaven.[4] If this did indeed come about from human affection, so much the more appropriate is it that I should plunge into the depths of thanksgiving; just as your condescension, my God, is greater in condescending to unite the gold of your inestimable worth to the clay of my worthlessness, so that the jewels of your graces might in this way find a place in me.

3. At the time I mentioned, when my mind was occupied with this subject with great devotion, I became aware that what I had just sought in the prayer I mentioned had been conferred on me, as if by divine intervention, utterly unworthy as I was. Inwardly in my heart, as if in physical places, I realized the Spirit had impressed the worshipful and adorable imprint of your most holy wounds. By those wounds you healed my soul and gave me the cup of the nectar of love to drink.

But my unworthiness had still not exhausted the depths of your loving-kindness, or prevented me from receiving this unforgettable gift from the overflowing abundance of your most generous

---

[2]Probably Mechtild of Hackeborn.
[3]Si 24:27.
[4]Ps 32(33):6.

munificence. As often as I concentrated on paying a daily visit, in spirit, to the tokens so lovingly imprinted, greeting them with five verses from [the psalm] 'Bless, my soul',[5] I never had grounds to complain that I had been cheated of a special blessing!

4. For at the first verse, 'Bless, my soul', I received the blessing of being able to lay down the rust of sin and the worthlessness of worldly sensuality at the wounds of your blessed feet. Then at the second verse, 'Bless, and forget not', I received the blessing of washing away every spot of carnal evanescent pleasure in the fountain of love from whence flowed blood and water[6] for me. At the third verse, 'He who is propitiated', I received the blessing of building my nest in the wound of your left hand for repose of spirit, while hastening to rest there like the dove in the rock.[7] Then at the fourth verse, 'Who redeems from the pit', I draw near to the right hand, and all that I lack in perfection of virtue is there deposited for me to claim as my own. When I am suitably adorned with these, at the fifth verse, 'Who fills with good things', may I who am now purified from all infamy of sin, and with my lack of merit made good, deserve to rejoice in your chaste embraces with your most desirable and most sweet presence. I am for my own part unworthy, but made worthy enough through you!

5. I declare that together with these blessings were conferred the requests made in that prayer, that I might read in those wounds your sorrow and your love alike. But to my great sorrow, though I cannot accuse you of having withdrawn this privilege from me, I mourn having shortly lost it through my own ingratitude and carelessness. But your great mercy and limitless loving-kindness, turning a blind eye, preserves to this very day that first, greater gift, the totally undeserved imprinting of your wounds, without any merit on my part. For this be honor and power, praise and rejoicing, through everlasting ages.

[5]Ps 102:1–5 / 103:1–5.
[6]Jn 19:34.
[7]Sg 2:14.

CHAPTER FIVE

THE WOUND OF LOVE

1. Six years later, before Advent, as you, Source of all good, had ordained, I had laid a certain person under an obligation to slip these words on my behalf into her daily prayer before the crucifix. She was to say, 'By your heart that was wounded through and through, most loving Lord, pierce her heart with the shafts of your love, so much so that it may be unable to possess anything that is of this earth, but may be possessed by the unique power of your divinity'. It was these prayers, I believe, that spurred you into action during Mass on the Sunday when 'Rejoice in the Lord'[1] is sung.

Out of the overflowing generosity of your goodness and by the permission of your mercy I was coming to receive the sacrament of your most holy body and blood, when you infused me with an earnest longing which compelled me to break out and say, 'Lord, I admit that, as far as my merits go, I am not worthy[2] to receive the least of your gifts. But by the merits and earnest longing of all those around I beseech your loving-kindness to pierce my heart with the arrow of your love'. Soon I became aware that the force of these words had reached your divine Heart, as much because of an inflow of inner grace as because

[1] The third Sunday of Advent.
[2] Mt 8:8.

112

of the manifestation of an unmistakable sign on an image of your crucifixion.

2. For when I had received the life-giving sacrament, and had returned to my place in choir, it seemed to me as if something like a ray of the sun came out from the right-hand side of the crucified Christ painted on the page, that is, from the wound in the side. It had a sharp point like an arrow and, astonishingly, it stretched forward and, lingering thus for a while, it gently elicited my love. But my longing was not thus satisfied until the following Wednesday when, after mass, the faithful honor the generous gift of your incarnation and annunciation, which all must adore.[3] I too, although less worthily, was concentrating on this devotion. Suddenly you were there unexpectedly, opening a wound in my heart with these words: 'May all your emotions come together in this place; that is may the sum total of your delight, hope, joy, sorrow, fear and your other emotions be fixed firmly in my love'.

3. I immediately remembered that I had sometimes heard that wounds should be washed, anointed and bound up. At that time you had not yet taught me, once and for all, how to do this. But after a while you revealed it more fully to me, by means of someone who to your praise, I believe, has attuned her inner ear much more reliably and more sensitively than I have, I am afraid, to catch the continual flow of your loving whispers. Her advice to me was that, while worshipping with constant devotion the love of your Heart hanging on the cross, I should draw water of devotion, to wash away every offence, from the moisture of charity produced by the burning heat of a love so indescribable. From the liquid of loving-kindness created by the sweetness of a love so incalculable, I should take the salve of thanksgiving, sovereign remedy against all adversity; and from the potent power of charity, perfected by the strength of a love so incomprehensible, I should find the binding

[3]That is, the recitation of the Angelus. The mass was that of the Ember Wednesday of Advent, which began *Missus est*.

of integrity, so that I might direct all my thoughts, words and deeds, given strength by love, toward you, and in this way cling inseparably to you.

4. May the power of that love whose fulness lives[4] in him who, sitting on your right hand,[5] has become bone of my bone and flesh of my flesh,[6] make up for whatever I have distorted as a result of my malice and wickedness in this account! For it is through him, in the power of the Holy Spirit, that you have given us this capacity, with nobility of compassion, humility and reverence. Through him too I offer you mourning for my far too numerous offences against your divinely noble goodness, which I have assaulted so variously, in thought, word and deed; but especially in that I made such faithless, careless and disrespectful use of the gifts of yours I have mentioned. For if you had handed over to me, unworthy as I am, a hempen thread in memory of yourself, I should rightly have treated it with more conscientious respect!

5. My God, you who know my secrets,[7] you know that this is the reason which compels me, reluctantly or rather against my will, to commit these experiences to writing: I consider that I have profited so little from them that I am unable to believe that they have been given me for myself alone, since your eternal wisdom cannot be set aside by anyone. Therefore, Giver of gifts,[8] you who have given me gifts so free and undeserved, give the reader of these words too the gift that the heart of your friend[9] may at least feel pity for you, in that your passion for souls has for so long confined a jewel worthy of a king to the muddy bilge-water of my heart! While offering prayer and thanksgiving, may [the reader] extoll your mercy and say with heart and mouth the antiphons *Te Deum patrem, Ex quo omnia, Te iure laudant, Tibi decus, Benedictio*

[4]Col 1:19.
[5]Col 3:1.
[6]Gn 2:23.
[7]Dan 13:42.
[8]From the Pentecost sequence 'Veni, Sancte Spiritus'.
[9]*amici tui*: see II, 20, note 3.

et claritas.[10] In this way some reparation may be made to you for my deficiency.

At this point she put off writing until October.

---

[10]The complete text of these antiphons, taken from the Office of the Holy Trinity, may be translated: 'With our whole heart and mouth we confess you, the Father unbegotten, you the only-begotten Son, and you the Holy Spirit and Paraclete, to be the Holy and Undivided Trinity, we praise you and bless you: to you be glory for ever.' 'From whom are all things, through whom are all things, in whom are all things: to him be glory for ever.' 'The whole creation rightly praises you, adores you and glorifies you, O blessed Trinity.' 'To you be honor and dominion, to you be glory and power, to you be praise and rejoicing, throughout all ages, O blessed Trinity.' 'Blessing and brightness and wisdom and thanksgiving, honor, power and strength be to our God for ever and ever. Amen.'

CHAPTER SIX

A MORE GRACIOUS VISITATION
OF THE LORD AT CHRISTMAS

1. O unattainable height[1] of marvellous power! O depth of the abyss of inscrutable wisdom! O immense breadth[2] of desirable love! How strongly swelled the ambrosial torrents of your honey-sweet divinity when they flooded me so fruitfully, worm of utter worthlessness that I am, squirming in the gravel of my sins of omission and commission! The outcome was that, to my great pleasure, even in my wandering exile I was allowed, in proportion to my ability, to experience again the foretaste of the most pleasing delights and sweetest pleasures, by which anyone who clings to God becomes one spirit with him.[3] The boundless nature of his blessedness, spread abroad so abundantly, permitted me, just a speck of dust, to have the audacity to lap up some of its droplets, in the way I shall describe.

---

[1] Rm 11:33.

[2] Eph 3:18. The first three sentences of this chapter suggest the making of the sign of the cross. The triune pattern of power, wisdom and love, ultimately derived from Augustine, is characteristically Bernardine: see *On Consideration* 13.

[3] 1 Co 6:17.

2. On that most holy of nights, when by the sweetening dew of divinity the heavens rained down honey[4] on the whole world, my soul, drenched like Gideon's fleece with dew on the threshing-floor[5] of the convent, was intent by meditation, and through the practice of certain devotions, on being present and offering help at the heavenly birth, at which the Virgin brought forth her son, true God and true man, like a ray of light.[6] As in a moment of revelation my soul realized that it had been offered, and had received, in place of its heart so to speak, a tender little boy. In him there lay hidden the gift of complete perfection, which is truly the best endowment.[7] When my soul cradled him within itself it suddenly seemed to be completely changed into the same color as him—if that can be called a 'color' which cannot be compared with any visible quality.

Then my soul perceived a meaning that defies explication in the sweet words, 'God shall be all in all'.[8] It felt that it held within itself the Beloved, installed in the heart, and it rejoiced that it was not without the welcome presence of its Spouse, with his most enjoyable caresses. Offered the honeyed draughts of the following, divinely inspired words, it drank them in with a thirst that could not be satisfied: 'Just as I bear the stamp of the substance of God the Father[9] in regard to my divine nature, so you bear the stamp of my substance in regard to my human nature, for you receive in your deified soul the outpourings of my divine nature, just as the air receives the sun's rays. Penetrated to the very marrow by this unifying force, you will become fit for a more intimate union with me'.

3. O noble balm of the divine, sending out streams of love on every side, flourishing and flowering for ever, but to be spread everywhere when time shall come to an end! O true power of the

---

[4]Second responsory for Christmas.

[5]Jg 6:39.

[6]A very common symbol of the virgin birth, taken from the sequence 'Laetabundus': 'Sicut sidus radium / Profert virgo filium'.

[7]Jm 1:17.

[8]1 Co 15:28.

[9]Heb 1:3.

invincible hand of the Most High, when a vessel so fragile and disgraced by its own imperfection contained so precious a liquid to be poured out![10] O proof most clear of the abundance of God's loving-kindness! It did not shrink from me, who wandered so far into the pathless wastes of my sins, but rather made known to me, as far as I was capable of it, the sweetness of that most blessed union!

---

[10]It would seem that the 'vessel' is human nature and the 'precious liquid' the incarnate Lord.

CHAPTER SEVEN

HER SOUL'S MORE EXALTED
UNION WITH GOD

1. Later, on the Feast of Candlemas, I was lying in bed after a serious illness. At sunrise I was silently mourning and lamenting that, held back by physical weakness, I was to be deprived of the divine visitation which had quite often given me strength on such a day. But then I was given consolation by the mediatrix of the Mediator of God and man:[1] 'Just as you do not remember having suffered a more bitter pang of sickness in your body, so you should know that you have never received a more noble gift from my Son, which your preceding physical sickness has strengthened your spirit to receive as it should be received'.

These words lifted a load from my heart. When it was time for the procession, after I had received the bread of life and was intent on God and myself, I realized that my soul, like wax[2] carefully softened in the fire, lay on the Lord's breast, as if about to be impressed with a seal. Suddenly it seemed to be seized and partially drawn into that treasury[3] in which the fullness of the divine dwells

[1] 1 Tm 2:5.
[2] Ps 21:15 / 22:15.
[3] *thesaurarium*, that is, the divine heart.

119

bodily,[4] and it was sealed with the indelible mark of the bright and ever-tranquil Trinity.

2. O devastating glowing coal,[5] my God, you who contain, radiate and brand with living heat! You exercised your inextinguishable power on my damp and slimy soul, first drying up in it the flood of worldly pleasures and afterwards softening the rigidity of its attachment to its own ideas, a position in which it had long been completely fixed. O truly devoring fire,[6] you who wield your power against vice so that you may reveal yourself to the soul gently when the time comes to anoint it! In you and in none other do we receive this strength,[7] so that we may have the power to be re-formed into the image and likeness[8] of our original state. O powerful furnace,[9] in the lovely vision of true peace,[10] by whose operation dross[11] is transformed into refined and choice gold when the soul, wearied by deceit, at long last blazes with an inner and insatiable desire to track down what belongs to it, and which it may receive from you alone, very Truth!

---

[4]Col 2:9.

[5]Ps 119:4 / 120:4.

[6]Dt 4:24; Heb 12:29.

[7]Ac 3:12.

[8]Gn 1:26; the phrase is a favorite of Saint Bernard's.

[9]Dan 3, *passim*.

[10]That is, in the heavenly Jerusalem, traditionally interpreted as 'the vision of peace'.

[11]Is 1:25.

CHAPTER EIGHT

[THE LORD'S] MORE INTIMATE
DEALING WITH HER

1. After this, on *Esto mihi* Sunday,[1] you stirred me up during mass and increased my longing for those more excellent gifts which you intended to confer on me. You did this in particular by means of two texts whose greater power I had earlier sensed in my soul, that is, the first responsory 'Blessing, I shall bless you',[2] and the ninth, 'For I shall give these lands to you and your seed....'.[3] At these words you touched your most blessed breast with your adorable hand and showed me the 'land' which your unrestrained generosity promised me.

2. O that blessed land which is a source of blessing, overflowing with blessedness! Field of delights, the smallest particle of your soil could satisfy and more than satisfy the hunger of all those whom you have chosen, in every single thing that the human heart could imagine as desirable, lovable, delightful, lovely and delicious! While I was concentrating on those things on which one should concentrate (if not as much as I should, at least as

[1]The Sunday before Ash Wednesday, until recently known as Quinquagesima Sunday.

[2]Compare Heb 6:14.

[3]Compare Gn 26:3.

much as I could) there appeared the goodness and humanity of God our Saviour! This was not the result of deeds of righteousness, as if I, unworthy that I am, could possibly have deserved it, but in virtue of his own ineffable mercy.[4] You were strengthening me by adoption and rebirth, and fitting me, most unworthy beyond the bounds of worthlessness, for something which should rightly strike us dumb and make us tremble but which we must worship and adore: a more potent union with yourself, transcending heaven and transcending human thought.

3 But to what merits of mine, to what decision of yours, my God, are we to attribute the fact that your love, heedless of its own riches but rich in condescension[5]—a precipitate love, I say, which does not wait for a judicious decision[6] and cannot be comprehended by human reason—that this love, my sweetest God, made you take leave of your senses (dare I say it?) as if you were drunk? In your madness you united two such total opposites. Or, to phrase it with greater dignity, the innate, natural loveliness of your goodness, utterly permeated with the sweetness of love, making you not merely a lover but wholly Love itself,[7] whose more natural flow you directed toward the salvation of humanity, persuaded you to summon the farthest-flung, most miserable specimen of the human race—one devoid of all gifts of grace and fortune, of despicable life and conduct—from the far reaches of her complete worthlessness to keep company with royal—no, divine—grandeur, so that every creature living on earth might grow in confidence. What I hope and desire for every Christian is that, because of the honor due to my Lord, no one may be found who is worse than I am when it comes to distorting God's gifts and scandalizing neighbors.

4. But since the invisible realities of God can be expressed to the outer understanding through created beings,[8] as I described it ear-lier the Lord made his appearance in that part of his blessed breast

[4]Tt 3:5.
[5]SC 64:10.
[6]SC 9:2.
[7]1 Jn 4:16.
[8]Rm 1:20.

in which he had, at Candlemas, received my soul like wax carefully softened in the fire. [My soul] was covered with little beads of sweat breaking out on it, as if the substance of that wax, shown to me earlier, had melted and liquefied because of the excessive heat hidden within. But the divine treasure-chest,[9] by some supernatural but indescribable, or rather unthinkable, power was absorbing these apparent beads of moisture, so that the overwhelming force that love there possessed was fully revealed where so great and impenetrable a secret was unlocked.

5. O eternal solstice, safe dwelling, place containing all pleasure, heavenly garden of everlasting delights flowing with streams of pleasures beyond price, coaxing forth the blossoming spring-time of all kinds of loveliness, soothing with sweet sound, or rather with the sweetly soothing sound of the affecting melody of spiritual music, bringing refreshment with the perfumed breath of life-giving scents, intoxicating with the melting sweetness of inner savors, bringing transformation with the wonderful caresses of intimate embraces! O thrice fortunate, four times blest, and, if I may say so, a hundred times holy are you who, prompted and guided by grace, have deserved to approach this place with innocent hands, a clean heart[10] and pure lips.

What sights, what sounds, what scents, what delicious savors, what sensations! But why does my stumbling tongue attempt to stammer them out? For though I am allowed to enter, thanks to the goodness of God (though still along the paths of my sins of omission and commission), I am as it were encased in a thick shell and am unable to catch at anything as it really is. For even if the combined abilities of human beings and angels could be concentrated into a single moment of worthy knowledge, it would not be adequate fully to express even a single word by which one could in the least degree worthily aspire to the sublimity of such great excellence.

---

[9]*gazophylacium*, that is Christ's breast, the 'treasure' being the divine heart.
[10]Ps 23:4 / 24:4.

CHAPTER NINE

THE INDISSOLUBLE
UNION OF HER SOUL

1. Quite soon afterwards, toward the middle of Lent, while I was confined to bed suffering once more from a serious illness, I was lying alone one morning as the other sisters were busy with other concerns. The Lord, who does not know how to abandon those abandoned by human comforts, was there present, proving the truth of the prophetic text 'I am with him in tribulation'.[1] For he extended from his left side, as if from the depths of his blessed Heart, a liquid stream of the purity and strength of crystal.[2] As it went forth it covered that adorable breast like a collar; it seemed translucent, tinted with gold and rosy pink, flickering between the two colors.[3]

While this was happening the Lord added, 'The sickness which causes you distress at present has sanctified your soul with the result that whenever, for my sake, you lower yourself to thoughts, words and deeds which are not concerned with me, you will never go further from me than is shown you in this stream. Moreover, just as it shines with gold and rosy pink through the purity of crystal, so the co-working of my golden divine nature and the perfect

[1]Ps 90:15 / 91:15.
[2]Rv 22:1.
[3]The effect would seem to be similar to shot silk.

patience of my rosy human nature[4] will be pleasing, suffusing and permeating all that you will'.

2. O the grandeur of that infinitesimal speck of dust, which the chief Jewel of the nobility of heaven takes out of the dusty chaff to place at his side! O the perfection of that tiny flower, which the sun's ray itself coaxes out of the swamps as if to make it shine out brightly! O the happiness of that fortunate and blessed soul, which the Lord of majesty considers worthy of so great a state! Although he is all-powerful in creating, nonetheless he created the soul—a soul, I mean, made lovely in his own image and likeness but still as far from him as the creation is from the Creator! And so a hundred times blessed is she who is granted the grace of continuing in such state—a state which, I am afraid, I have never attained even for a moment. But I earnestly wish that the mercy of God will grant me the gift of such a grace by the merits of those whom, I hope, he has preserved in such a state for some length of time.

3. O gift that is above every gift,[5] to be satisfied so abundantly in the store-room by the sweet scents of the divine! and in the wine-cellar,[6] hutch of pleasure, to become so overflowingly drunk on the wine of love, even to be drowned,[7] so that one is not suffered to take the slightest step toward those distant lands where the power of such fragrance is likely to grow faint! Not only that: as often as it might be necessary to travel there under the guidance of love, what a gift it is to carry with one the lingering aftertaste of such total satisfaction, that one may be able to offer sweet odors from the divine richness of abundant sweetness!

I have complete confidence, Lord God, that out of the strength of your omnipotence you have the power to grant this gift to those whom you have chosen. And I do not doubt that you wished to grant it to me out of your loving goodness. As to how you could

---

[4]See C. Joret, *La rose dans l'antiquité et au moyen âge* (Paris, 1892, repr. Geneva, 1970), pp. 242–4, on the associations of the rose with Christ and his passion.

[5]Ph 2:9.

[6]Sg 1:3.

[7]This passage is possibly inspired by Ps 35:9 / 36:9.

grant it to me in spite of my unworthiness, I am totally unable to penetrate your unsearchable wisdom.[8]

But now I glorify and magnify your wise and kindly omnipotence. I praise and adore your omnipotent and kindly wisdom. I give blessings and thanks to your omnipotent and wise kindliness, my God, for no matter what you could ever have bestowed on me, I have always received incalculably more than I deserve from your generosity.

[8]Si 1:3.

CHAPTER TEN

THE INFLUENCE OF GOD

1. As I considered it so inappropriate to write down this account, I could not come to any agreement with my conscience on the subject and I had put off a decision until the Feast of the Exaltation of the Holy Cross.[1] On that day it was my firm intention to concentrate on other matters during mass, but the Lord guided my understanding toward these words: 'You may know for certain that you will never leave the prison of the flesh until you pay out that final penny[2] which until now you have held back'. I was meditating on the fact that I had written down everything that he had mentioned—or even if I not actually written it, I had nonetheless made restitution by my words, with my neighbors' profit in mind. But the Lord put in my way the verse which I had heard read at Lauds that very night: 'If the Lord had given nothing but oral teaching to those who were present, there would only have been sayings, not writings; but now they have in addition been written down, for the salvation of many'. The Lord added: 'Do not cross me! It is my wish to have in your writings irrefutable evidence of my divine loving-kindness for these last days, when I plan to bestow blessings on many'.

[1] 14 September.
[2] Mt 5:26.

127

2. Overwhelmed by this, I began to ponder how difficult or even impossible it would be for me to find expressions or words with which his many sayings could be brought forth, without shocking human understanding. The Lord, aware of my faint heart, seemed to drench my soul with a most generous shower of rain. Its heavy fall beat down on me, miserable scrap of humanity that I am, a delicate and tender little shoot, and flattened me to the ground. I could absorb nothing of any use except some profoundly significant words which I could not grasp with my human understanding. Completely overwhelmed by this, I asked what could come of these words? Your usual loving-kindness, my God, gently lightened this burden and refreshed my soul with these words: 'Since you found the rushing flood of those torrents of no use, I shall now draw you to my divine heart so that I may flow gently and sweetly into you, rhythmically, and proportioned to your capacity'.

3. I declare this promise was absolutely true, because of its complete fulfilment, O Lord God. Every day for four days continuously, early in the morning at the best time, you inspired me with a part of the discourse recorded above,[3] so clearly and so gently that, without any mental effort, I was able to write without any previous thought, just as if I had learnt it by heart long ago. You did this, however, with such restraint that when I had written down a suitable section, however much I cudgelled my brains, I could not run to earth one more of those phrases which on the next day would spring to mind in such effortless abundance. Throughout, you somehow controlled and bridled my impetuosity—just as Scripture teaches[4] that no one should be so wedded to action as not to show any desire for contemplation. Being always consumed with a passion for my salvation, you grant me leisure to rejoice in the lovely embraces of Rachel, but you do not allow me to lose the glorious fecundity of Leah. May your wise love allow both to achieve perfection in a way that pleases you.

[3]That is, Bk II. 6–9.
[4]Lk 10:41.

CHAPTER ELEVEN

AN ASSAULT BY TEMPTATION

1. How often, and in how many different guises, have you communicated the sensation of your saving presence to me! In what an immense blessing of sweetness[1] have you consistently gone before me in my littleness, especially during the first three years, but more especially whenever I am permitted to share in your blessed body and blood. Since I am totally incapable of answering once in a thousand times,[2] I trust in that everlasting, immense and unchanging goodness by which, O shining ever-tranquil Trinity, all that is owing is paid to you in full out of your own resources, by them and in them. I fling myself, like a tiny speck of dust,[3] on this mercy, through him who sits at your right hand while sharing my nature.[4] I offer you the thanks that you have made possible through him, in the Holy Spirit, for all your benefits; I thank you especially for having made me understand, stupid as I am, by means of a clear demonstration, how I was corrupting the purity of your gifts.

[1]Ps 20:4 / 21:4.
[2]Jb 9:3.
[3]Is 40:15.
[4]From the proper *Communicantes* in the mass of the Ascension.

129

2. For once, when I was attending mass and about to receive communion, and was aware that you were there in supernatural condescension, you used this analogy to teach me how you were asking me for a refreshing drink,[5] like a thirsty man. When I complained that I did not have one and had proved conclusively that I could not squeeze out even a single drop, it seemed to me as if your hands offered me a golden cup. When I had taken it, my heart dissolved in sweetness and out of it burst a flood of fervent tears. While this was happening, there sat at my left hand a loathsome creature who was surreptitiously putting something poisonous and bitter into my hand and forcing me, secretly but earnestly, to poison the wine in the cup with it. There soon followed an immense outbreak of vainglory, so that I was permitted to understand clearly what deception the ancient Adversary uses in his fight against us, out of envy for your gifts.

3. But thanks be to your faithfulness, my God, and to your protective care, true and single Divinity, single and three-fold Truth, three-fold and single Deity, which does not allow us to be tempted beyond our capacity.[6] For whenever you grant the enemy the power to tempt us, to test our progress, if you see that we are trustingly relying on your help, you take upon yourself the struggle planned for us. You do this to such a degree that, reserving the fight for yourself, out of your most abundant generosity you credit us with the victory as long as we cling to you with the intention of our will. And what is outstanding among your gifts is that, to increase our merit, your grace preserves the freedom of our will. You do not allow the Adversary to take it away, nor do you too have the desire to do so.

4. Another time, however, you taught me by another image that in any matter in which someone gives way too easily to our Adversary, the door is opened for a more powerful assault by him, since the perfection of your justice demands that you sometimes hide the power of your mercy in areas which our own neglect has

[5]Jn 4:7.
[6]1 Co 10:13.

made more vulnerable. And so the more prompt our resistance to any evil whatsoever, the more effective, profitable and potentially successful it is.

CHAPTER TWELVE

BEARING WITH HUMAN INADEQUACY

1. I thank you, just as I did earlier, for another similar image which was no less welcome and useful. By it you showed me how your kindly patience bears with our inadequacies so that, when we have remedied them, you may be able to raise us to a state of blessedness.

2. For one evening I had been in a state of anger; the next morning there was a chance to pray before sunrise. You appeared to me in the form of a vagrant, so that I might judge from your appearance that you were completely forlorn, bereft of possessions and power. Then my conscience, guilty because of its recent lapse, gnawed at me and lamenting I began to ponder how outrageous it was to be a trouble to you, the source of perfect purity and peace, with the stings of the vices that disturb me. I judged it to be more proper, or rather I made up my mind that it was preferable, for you to take your departure rather than be present at that very moment when I had failed to repell the Adversary, who was driving me into actions so contrary to you.

At this I received the following reply: 'If a sick man has, with difficulty, made his way outside with others' help to enjoy the splendid sunshine which he likes so much, what comfort can he have when a sudden storm blows up, except the hope of a return of the earlier fair weather? In the same way I, laid low by my love for you, choose to make my home with you amid all the squalls of your faults, setting my course for the calm of repentance and the harbor of humility'.

3. Since the power of speech cannot expound how you have distinguished me more abundantly in this revelation through the continued possession of such a gift,[1] I pray that my heart's love may go forward, and that out of the abyss of humiliation into which the condescension of your love drew me more powerfully, it may teach me to direct the effect of my thanksgiving toward the affect of your loving-kindness.[2]

---

[1] That is, the gift of her continual sense of the divine presence.
[2] *gratitudinis effectum . . . pietatis affectum.*

CHAPTER THIRTEEN

THE CUSTODY OF THE AFFECTIONS

1. Once more I give thanks to your loving-kindness, most kindly God, for in yet another way you intervened to arouse me from my inertia. Although you had initiated it through an intermediary, you brought it to fruition in person, acting both mercifully and courteously. The intermediary was explaining to me that, according to the gospel, when you were born on earth shepherds were the first to find you. She added that you had passed this message to her, that if I really wished to find you, I should pay attention to 'keeping watch' over my senses, just as the shepherds kept watch over their flocks.[1]

I did not welcome this advice, and considered it completely inapplicable to me since I knew you had not dealt with me as if I were serving you as a hired shepherd serves his master.[2] This thought preoccupied me from morning until night and I became depressed. After Compline, when I retreated to my place of prayer you assuaged my sorrow by means of this guiding thought. If a wife is sometimes busy procuring food for her husband's falcons, this does not mean that she is completely deprived of his embraces. Similarly if I worked at the custody of my affections and senses for your sake, I would not, for that reason, be deprived of the

[1]Lk 2:8, 16.
[2]Jn 10:11–12.

sweetness of your grace. For this purpose you gave me the spirit of fear[3] under the form of a green staff with which, without leaving your close embraces even a little, I could feel my way through all the border-lands of uncharted territory where human affections have a habit of straying.

You also added that whenever anything should slip in which threatened to lead any of my affections astray—whether to the right, as joy and hope, or to the left, as fear, sorrow or anger—I would instantly drive back that affection with the staff of your fear and, by disciplining my senses, I would cook that affection in the heat of my heart and serve it up as a feast for you, like a tender newborn lamb!

How often, when at the instigation of evil I have in word or deed allowed some gift I had formerly offered up to you, when there was an opportunity, to escape through euphoria or depression, I have seen myself snatching that gift away from you (as if I were pulling out your teeth) and offering it to your enemy! In the midst of all this you would seem to look at me with such kindly serenity as if you, being completely incapable of deceit yourself, thought that I was doing this as a gesture of affection! Hence you have so often led me out of such a state to so great a sweetness of loving agitation that I do not believe you could ever, by terrifying me with threats, induce me to long so much to correct and keep careful watch over myself.

[3]Is 11:3.

CHAPTER FOURTEEN

WHAT COMPASSION CAN ACHIEVE

1. Once, before Lent, on the Sunday when the introit is *Esto mihi*,[1] you granted me the grace of understanding that, abused and harassed by all and sundry, you were asking me through the words of that introit for a dwelling place to rest in. For the next three days, whenever I returned to my heart I saw you in the likeness of a sick man reclining on my breast. During those three days I did not find any meal I could serve you that was more gladly received than my being constant in prayer, silence and other penitential practices offered in reparation for those leading worldly lives, for the sake of your honor.[2]

[1]See note 1 to Book II.8:1.
[2]Compare Augustine, *Confessions* VII, 10.

CHAPTER FIFTEEN

REPAYING GOD'S GRACE

1. Similarly, as the grace of your loving-kindness illuminates my understanding, you have revealed to me many times how the soul, as long as it remains in its body of human weakness, is in darkness, like someone who stands in the middle of a confining room. From every side, around, above and below, it is assaulted by the haze the room gives off, just as a boiling pan gives off steam. On the other hand, when the body happens to be afflicted by some suffering, in relation to the suffering organ the soul receives something like a breath of fresh air shot through and through with sunlight, and is granted light in this supernatural way. And the more all-embracing or the more serious the suffering, the purer the enlightenment of the soul. But, more particularly, affliction and the disciplining of the heart in humility, patience and the like, tint the soul with a dazzling whiteness in so far as these practices touch it more closely, effectively and intimately. But it becomes especially calm and radiant from works of charity.

2. Thanks be to you, Lover of men and women, for so often drawing me towards patience in this way. But alas! a thousand times alas! that I have given you my consent so little and so rarely—or rather, not at all as I should have done. Lord, you know the sorrow, confusion and dejection of my spirit over this, and the

desire of my heart that I should make up for my shortcomings toward you in some other way.

Again, when on one occasion I was about to receive communion at mass, you had bestowed your riches rather generously and I sought to discover what I could do in my turn to repay you for a fraction at least of your condescension. You, most wise of teachers, put before me the words of Saint Paul: 'I wished to be condemned and cut off for the sake of my brothers'.[1] At that moment, when thanks to your prompting, I had known that my heart was the dwelling-place of my soul, you then showed me that my soul also had a dwelling-place in the head; afterwards, I declare that I realized this from the evidence of Scripture, although I had not known it before. You explained to me how it is a great deed if the soul gives up the sweetness of the heart's fulfilment for your sake, keeps vigil in governing its bodily senses and labors over works of charity for the salvation of its neighbors as well.

[1]Rm 9:3.

CHAPTER SIXTEEN

GRACIOUS REVELATIONS AT CHRISTMAS AND CANDLEMAS

1. On the day of your most holy Nativity, I took you from the manger as a tiny child wrapped in swaddling clothes.[1] You were imprinted on my innermost heart, so that I might gather together a bundle of myrrh from all the bitter humiliations of childhood's need[2] to linger between my breasts,[3] and thence might press and drink from the cluster of grapes of divine sweetness in the depths of my being. Although I reckoned I could never receive any gift greater than this, you, who so often follow up what has gone before with an even nobler gift, condescended to embroider on the theme of the overflowing abundance of your saving grace in the following way.

2. The next year, on the same day, during the mass *Dixit Dominus*,[4] I took you from the lap of your virgin mother in the shape of a most tender and delicate little child. While I was carrying you on my bosom, it seemed to me that the sympathy I had shown someone in trouble before Christmas by offering special prayers

[1]Lk 2:8.
[2]SC 43.3.
[3]Sg 1:12–13.
[4]Ps 2:7, the introit for the midnight mass of Christmas.

was at work here too. But I have to say that even though I had that gift, to my sorrow I was not as ardent in my devotion as I should have been. I do not know whether it was your justice or my carelessness that was responsible for this. It was my hope however that your justice, with the help of your mercy, had so disposed things that on the one hand my worthlessness might be made known the more clearly to me, and on the other that I might be filled with fear that my carelessness was to blame, in that I was too sluggish in rejecting vain thoughts. Whatever the reason, you must answer on my behalf, O Lord my God.[5]

Now as I was collecting myself somewhat to fondle you with loving caresses, I realized that I had made little progress until I recited prayers for sinners, souls in purgatory and those otherwise troubled. I was soon aware of the result of these prayers, especially when one evening I decided to pray with all departed souls in mind. Up until then I had made an intention for my parents with the collect, 'God, you have commanded us to honor our father and mother'; so by extension I made an intention for those dear to you with the collect, 'Almighty and everlasting God, to whom never without hope....' It seemed to me that you took greater pleasure in this. Moreover you seemed to take a sweet delight in it when, putting all my efforts into singing, I fixed my intention on you at every single note, just like someone who carefully keeps her eye on the book because she is singing without the thorough knowledge that comes from long experience. How many things I neglected in these matters, and in others I knew to be done for your praise, I confess to you, most kindly Father, in the bitterness of the passion of your guiltless son Jesus Christ, in whom you testified that you took greatest pleasure when you said, 'This is my beloved son, in whom I am well pleased'.[6] Through him I offer my amendment of life, so that through him all that I have failed to do, may be made good.

3. Then on the most holy day of Candlemas, when we celebrate that procession in which you chose to be brought into the Temple with the other sacrificial victims as our salvation and redemption,

[5]Is 38:14.
[6]Mt 17:5.

in the course of the antiphon *Cum inducerent* your Virgin Mother
asked me with an air of severity to give her back the dear little
child of her womb as if I had not looked after you as well as she
wished—you who are the honor and the joy of spotless viginity
itself.[7] Remembering that because she found favor in your sight
she had been given as their reconciliation to sinners and as their
hope to all people in despair, I burst out and said, 'O Mother
of loving-kindness, surely the living spirit of mercy[8] was given to
you as your son for this purpose, that you might win mercy for all
those in need of grace, and that your boundless love might cover
over the multitude of our sins and shortcomings'.[9]

At this, the expression of that kindly lady became calm and
merciful and she showed that, although she had seemed severe
since my evil demanded it, her inmost being was nonetheless brim-
ful of love, and that she was suffused through and through with
the sweetness of divine love. Soon her face grew radiant while, at
my feeble words, the severity she had shown vanished and a tran-
quil sweetness, her innate characteristic, shone forth. May your
mother's generous loving-kindness act as gracious intercessor in
the presence of your mercy for all my shortcomings!

4. Finally it became clearer than daylight that you could not contain the overflowing abundance of your sweetness. The next year,
on the same holy feast, you graced me with a gift more welcome
than the one I have mentioned but not unlike it. It was just as
if my attentive devotion had earned it from you the year before,
although in all justice I had earned, not another gift but rather a
fitting punishment for having lost the earlier one! For while they
were reading the gospel, 'She brought forth her first-born son...'[10]
with her spotless hands your spotless mother proffered me you, the
child of her virginity, a loveable baby struggling with all his might
to be embraced by me. I (though to my sorrow most undeserving) took you, a fragile little child, who clung to me with your
little arms. I became aware of such life-giving refreshment from

[7] Th 2:19, from the Preface of the ritual for the consecration of virgins.
[8] From the antiphon 'Salve virginale palatium'.
[9] 1 P 4:8.
[10] Lk 2:7, from the gospel read at the midnight mass of Christmas.

the breath of the sweetly-flowing spirit coming from your blessed mouth that my soul should, in all justice, bless you from that moment forward, and all that is within me should bless your holy name.[11]

5. While your blessed mother was busy wrapping you in a child's swaddling clothes, I was asking to be wrapped in them with you, lest you should be separated from me by even so much as a thin piece of cloth! For your embraces and kisses far surpass draughts of honey. Thus I saw you wrapped in the pure white linen of innocency, and bound by the golden bands of love; if I wished to be wrapped and bound in them with you, I was obliged above all to work wholeheartedly at purity of heart and works of loving charity.

6. Thanks be to you, who made the stars and dressed the bright heavens[12] and all the varied flowers of spring! Though you had no need of anything in my possession,[13] yet with my instruction in mind you asked me after this, on the feast of Candlemas, to dress you, little child that you were, before you were taken to the Temple. You persuaded me, out of the secret treasury of divine inspiration, to carry out this task in the following way.

With all my might I was struggling to praise the spotless innocence of your most pure human nature with such complete and faithful devotion that, if I could have had in my own person all glory, I would have freely made it over (as would be right and proper) to your kindly innocence, so that I might make you yet more praiseworthy in your innocence. As a result of such an intention on my part, I saw you dressed in white garments like a little child—you whose omnipotence summons those things that are not as much as those that are.[14] While with similar devotion I contemplated the depth of your humility, I saw you wearing also a green tunic, to symbolize the fact that your grace which has burst into flower is always alive and vital, and never dries up

[11]Ps 102:1 / 103:1.

[12]From the hymn 'Conditor alme siderum' in the Advent office.

[13]Ps 15:2 / 16:2.

[14]Rm 4:17.

in the valley of humility. Next, when I recollected in the same
way as before the motive which spurred you on in all that you
did, you were wrapped round with a purple cloak to show that
love is a truly regal garment, without which no one may enter
the kingdom of heaven.[15]

While I praised, as far as I could, the same virtues in your
glorious mother I saw her too dressed in the same way. And since
this blessed Virgin, the rose that blossoms without a thorn,[16] the
white lily without spot, abounds—abounds to overflowing—with
the flowers of every variety of virtue, we pray that she may act
as our eternal mediator,[17] that through her our poverty may be
transformed into riches.

[15]Mt 22:12–13.
[16]From the sequence 'Ave Maria'.
[17]Antiphon 'Gaude Dei genetrix'.

CHAPTER SEVENTEEN

THE DIVINE SELF-RESTRAINT

1. One day, when I had washed my hands and was about to go to eat, I was standing around with the other members of the community and noticed the brilliance of the sun shining with all its strength. This gave me pause for thought, and I said to myself, 'If the Lord who created that sun and at whose beauty it is said that the sun itself and the moon are filled with wonder,[1] the Lord who is also a consuming fire,[2] were really and truly with me as he so often presents himself to me, how could it possibly be that I could lead my life among human beings with such a chilly heart, and so devoid of human warmth, or rather, so full of evil?'

All at once you, whose words, always sweet,[3] were at that moment even sweeter as being more necessary to my wavering heart, put these words into my mind: 'How could my almighty power receive its due of praise if it were not possible for me, wherever I might be, to remain within myself so as not to appear or be perceived beyond what is most appropriate for the place, the time and the individual? From the beginning of the creation of heaven and earth, throughout the labor of redemption, I have made greater use of kindly wisdom than of majestic

[1]Office of Saint Agnes.
[2]Dt 4:24; Heb 12:29.
[3]Sg 4:3.

force. This kindly wisdom shines forth with greatest power in my forbearance towards those who are less than perfect, going so far as to lead them, through their free will, to the path of perfection'.

CHAPTER EIGHTEEN

FATHERLY TEACHING

1. One feast day, while I noticed that that a number of women were going up for communion who had entrusted themselves to my prayers, I was myself held back by physical weakness—or rather driven away, I am afraid, at divine instigation by my unworthiness, —and called to mind the many blessings, God, that you had given me. I began to fear that the wind of vainglory might be able to dry up the floods of divine grace, and I longed to be imbued with insight which would fortify me for the future. Then your fatherly loving-kindness taught me that I should judge your affection for me to be like that of the father of a family, who takes a real joy in the graceful poise of his numerous children, on whom a vast crowd of relatives and neighbors congratulate him. Among them he has a little child who has not yet achieved the poise of the rest, but in his fatherly love he feels sorry for it, clasps it to his bosom more often, and spoils it more than the others with kind words and little presents. You also added that if I genuinely considered myself to be less perfect than others, the torrential flood of your honey-sweet divine nature[1] would never cease to flow into my soul.

2. I give thanks to you, my most loving God, lover of men and women, through that reciprocal movement of thanksgiving to and

[1]Ps 35:9 / 36:9.

146

fro within the Trinity, ever to be worshipped and adored, for this and for many other salutary demonstrations which you, the best of teachers, have used on many occasions to educate me, fool that I am. In the bitterness of the passion of Jesus Christ I move my plea,[2] offering up to you his sufferings and tears for all my acts of negligence which have stifled your sweetly-flowing Spirit[3] within me. In union with that most potent prayer of that same beloved Son in the power of the Holy Spirit, I ask you to amend all my sins and make up all my inadequacies. May you condescend to grant me this, through that love which restrained you when the most loving only son of your fatherly tenderness was counted among criminals.[4]

---

[2]*moveo querimoniam: querimonia* has the technical legal sense of 'plaint, plea, suit, especially one instituted without writ'.

[3]Ws 12:1.

[4]Is 53:12.

CHAPTER NINETEEN

IN PRAISE OF THE DIVINE GENEROSITY

1. I give thanks to your kindly mercy and merciful kindness, most loving Lord, for the proof you have revealed of your most generous loving-kindness. By this you settled my unstable and wavering mind when, as was my custom, I begged with incessant longing to be released from the prison of this wretched flesh.[1] It was not my purpose to avoid experiencing further wretchedness, but that your goodness might be released from that debt of grace which you are obliged to pay me in full, a debt in which the powerful love of your own divine nature entangled you, for the sake of the salvation of my soul. Not that you, who are divine Omnipotence and eternal Wisdom, could be constrained by necessity to give anything against your will. No, it is rather that out of the overflowing generosity of your loving-kindness you were making payment to a woman who was totally undeserving and gave you no thanks.

For you, splendor and crown of heavenly glory,[2] seemed to come down from the imperial throne of your majestic state in a most sweet and gentle downward flight. Throughout the length and breadth of heaven this journey shed what appeared to be streams of a most sweet liquid, to which every single one of the

[1]Rm 7:24.
[2]1 Th 2:19.

saints gladly bent down and, as if drinking the nectar of that torrential flood[3] with joyful pleasure, burst into a song praising God, delightful to hear. Amidst this I heard these words: 'Consider how sweetly this praise penetrates the ears of my divine majesty, and reaches the molten core of my loving Heart. No more are you to long so persistently to be released because you do not wish, while living in the flesh, to be the recipient of a gift of freely-given loving-kindness such as I lavish on you. For the more unworthy the one to whom I condescend, the greater the reverence with which I am rightly glorified by the whole of creation'.

2. Since I had been granted this experience at the moment when I was approaching your life-giving sacrament, I was therefore, quite properly, concentrating on it. You then granted me, in addition to the revelation I have just described, this moment of understanding: that everyone ought to approach the most sacred sharing of your body and blood in this way and with this intention: for love of the sacrament they should discount their love of your glory even to the extent, if it is possible, of receiving in that sacrament their own condemnation.[4] Then the divine loving-kindness may shine out the more, in that God did not disdain to give himself in communion to someone so unworthy.

When, however, I brought forward the objection that those who abstain from communion because of their own unworthiness, abstain with the intention of not bringing dishonour on so exalted a sacrament by their presumption, I received your blessed answer to this as follows: 'No one could ever come to communion irreverently who relied on an intention such as that'. For this be praise and glory to you for ever and ever!

[3]Compare Ps 35:9 / 36:9.
[4]1 Co 11:29.

CHAPTER TWENTY

SPECIAL PRIVILEGES
CONFERRED ON HER BY GOD

1. May my heart and my soul, together with the whole substance of my flesh and all the powers and faculties of my body and spirit along with the whole created world, give praise and thanksgiving unto you, sweetest God, most faithful lover of human salvation, for your most generous mercy! Your loving-kindness was not content merely to ignore the fact that I had the temerity to approach so many times the most excellent feast of your most holy body and blood improperly prepared. Your inexhaustible superabundance toward me, the most worthless and useless of your instruments, condescended to tinge your gift with added beauty: from your grace I received an assurance that if anyone who longs to approach the blessed sacrament but has a fearful conscience and holds back in trepidation is prompted by humility to seek support and strength from me, the very least of your servants: for the sake of that humility your loving-kindness, which bursts all bonds of restraint, will count them as worthy of so great a sacrament, which they will indeed receive as the fruit of eternal salvation. You added that if your absolute righteousness would not allow you to count someone worthy, you would never allow that person to submit in humility to my counsel.

O heavenly Governor, you who dwell on high and look down on the lowly,[1] how can it be that your divine compassion should pass such a decree, when you saw me so often approaching communion unworthily and, if weighed in the balance of your justice, deserving judgment! You wished to make others worthy by means of the power of humility, even though you could do this better without me. Nonetheless your loving-kindness, aware of my poverty, made the decision to accomplish this through me, so that in this way if in no other I could have a share in the merits of those who would, through my words of advice, come to possess the fruit of salvation.

2. But since, to my great sorrow, this is not the only respect in which my wretched state leaves much to be desired, your compassion, kindly God, was not content with a single remedy alone. For this reason you also gave me, most unworthy though I am, this assurance: if any with contrite heart and humbled spirit[2] uncover with deep grief some shortcoming for me to see, and then hear from me whether that shortcoming is serious or trivial, you, merciful God, are willing to judge them more guilty or more innocent according to my words. From that time onwards they would always enjoy relief through your mediating grace in that they would never be so dangerously oppressed by that shortcoming as before. In this too you were aware of my most wretched poverty so that I, who all my life have been so negligent that I have never, to my great sorrow, gained the mastery over even the least of my shortcomings as I should, might at least deserve to have a share in the victories of others. For you, my God and my Good, condescended to adopt me as a most unworthy instrument for this purpose, that through the words of my mouth you might transmit the grace of victory to other more worthy friends of yours.[3]

---

[1] Ps 112:5–6 / 113:5–6.

[2] Dan 3:39; compare the prayer of oblation (*Suscipe*) in the offertory of the mass.

[3] *amicis tuis*: Mechtild of Magdebourg uses the phrase 'auserwählter Gottesfreunde' for all those striving for perfection in a hostile and secular milieu. In the fourteenth century the phrase 'Friends of God' came to be associated with Eckhart, Suso and their followers, but also with various heretical and apocalyptic movements: see *Oxford Dictionary of the Christian Church*, *s. v.* 'Gottesfreunde'.

3. Thirdly, the liberal generosity of your grace also enriched my lack of merit with this assurance: if I, relying on the divine loving-kindness, had promised someone a blessing or pardon for some fault, your kindly love would determine to hold to my words as steadfastly as if you had sworn it in truth with your own blessed mouth. So truthfully did you make this promise that you added that if people thought that the promised favor which would advance their salvation was deferred longer than they wished, they should bring it to your attention by constantly reminding you that I had promised them salvation on your behalf. In this way you make provision for my own salvation, according to the words of the gospel, 'In the same measure as you have measured will it be measured out to you'.[4] As a result since, to my great sorrow, I cannot cease from falling often into serious sin, you at least have the opportunity of judging my sins more leniently.

4. Fourthly, you added another necessary blessing, assuring me among other things that any who entrusted themselves to my prayers with humility and devotion would without any doubt gain all the profit they believed they would gain through the prayers of another. In this too you showed your awareness of my negligence, for I completely fail to perform the prayers of the Church, both those that are obligatory and those that are voluntary, from which I could myself draw riches, according to the text 'Your prayer shall return to your own bosom'.[5] But you would allow me to have a share, through sharing a little in the fragments that remain in the harvest of those whom you have chosen, whom you blessed when they asked through me, most unworthy though I am.

5. Fifthly, you did not refrain from furthering my salvation in another way, in that you conferred on me, as a sort of special gift, the grace that all those who with good will, right purpose and humble trust discuss their spiritual progress with me, will never leave me without edification or spiritual consolation. It was as if you anticipated that this was in keeping with my poverty, since often, to my great sorrow, I talk on and on to little purpose and,

[4]Lk 6:38.
[5]Ps 34:13 / 35:13.

so to speak, scatter all over the ground the talent for articulate expression which your generosity has entrusted to my unworthy keeping.[6] But at least I may scrape together from someone else's hoard some small profit of spiritual riches.

6. Sixthly, your generosity, kindly God, gave me another gift which is altogether essential. You gave me an assurance that any who of their charity prayed for me, most worthless of God's creatures, with devotion and faith, or even offered prayers and good works as recompense for the ignorant faults of my youth[7] — or rather my malice and wickedness[8] — would receive this reward, the gift of your most generous loving-kindness: that they would not die before the granting of this grace, that their way of life would find such favor in your sight that you could take some uniquely intimate delight in their soul. This is the result of your most kind and fatherly nature and also of my great need, since you knew very well how extensive and many-faceted was my need for correction, for so many innumerable faults and failures.[9] Your loving compassion would by no means allow me to perish but, on the other hand, the beauty of your justice could by no means permit me, with my so many different failures, to be saved; by this means if by no other provision was made for me that by sharing in the riches of many, the riches of the one might increase.

7. Out of your unbounded generosity, kindly God, you made yet another addition to all this. If any should come to realize, after my death, how your intimate companionship had so graciously favored my poor self during my lifetime and for this reason should be willing humbly to entrust themselves to my prayers, unworthy though they are, you would certainly be willing to pay heed to them with great generosity, just as you would be willing to pay heed to anyone through the prayers of someone else. In reparation for my negligence they have only to give you thanks with humble devotion for five things in particular:

[6]Mt 25: 14–28.
[7]Ps 24:7 / 25:7.
[8]1 Co 5:8.
[9]Prayer of oblation (*Suscipe*) in the offertory of the mass.

8. First, for the love which led your freely-given loving-kindness to choose me from the beginning of time. To tell the truth, this is the most freely-given of gifts, before all others. You know the story of my misguided way of life, and in particular my malice and wickedness and my vicious ingratitude, to such an extent that you could justly have refused to honor me with human reason, along with unbelievers. But your loving-kindness, which far surpasses my ills,[10] chose me in preference to other Christians to be stamped with the seal of the religious life.

9. Secondly, you drew me to yourself for my salvation. This too I declare in all justice is a manifestation of your intrinsic gentleness and kindness, since you drew my unruly heart[11] to yourself with sweet caresses, a heart which was, in strict equity, fit only for iron fetters. It was as if you had found in me a partner in your own gentleness, and delighted in being joined to me in all things.

10. Third, you granted me an intimate union with yourself. This too I must ascribe, most justly, to the utterly unrestrained superabundance of your generosity. As if the number of the righteous were not enough to receive the excess of your loving-kindness, you condescended to call on me who least deserved it, not that you might justify (an easy task) one already advanced in the spiritual life, but that the miracle of your condescension might blaze the brighter in one who was less adept.

11. Fourth, you take a deep pleasure in this union. This too I ascribe to your (dare I say it?) mad love. You have not disdained to assert that it is this that you call your 'delighted enjoyment', that your omnipotent Wisdom takes pleasure in the fact that she can sometimes, in so incredible a way, enter into union with a being so totally unlike herself and in all ways completely unfit!

12. Fifth, you condescended to bring me to the blessed state of perfection. I humbly and firmly hope that, by the faithful promise of your truth, I though most unworthy will receive that blessing

---

[10]From 'Jesu nostra redemptio', sung at vespers of the Ascension.
[11]Ezk 2:4.

from the most sweet loving-kindness of your most merciful love, and I embrace that hope with gratitude and a totally confident love. It is not thanks to any merits of my own but solely through the spontaneous clemency of your compassion, O my highest, or rather my only, entire, true and eternal Good![12]

13. Since all these individual gifts of your astounding generosity are so completely out of keeping with my insignificance that there is no way in which I could give you sufficient thanks, in this too you came to the aid of my poverty. By your kind promises you led others to thanksgiving, whose merits can fill out and make up for my own inadequacies. For this be praise appropriate to your generosity, and thanksgiving, on behalf of all things in heaven, on earth and under the earth.[13]

14. Above and beyond all this, my God, the priceless power of your love[14] bestowed another gift, the most gracious confirmation and ratification of the gifts already described. For one day while meditating on them and comparing your loving-kindness with my own lack of love, I was filled with joy that the one so surpassed the other, so much so that I was swept away into a rash complaint that you had not confirmed them in the way that those entering on a contract usually do, that is by shaking hands! Your most pliant sweetness kindly promised to meet these objections, saying, 'Don't complain! Come and receive the official confirmation of my covenant with you'.

At once, insignificant as I am, I saw you open up as if with both hands that ark of divine constancy and infallible truth, that is, your deified Heart. I saw you commanding me, since I was so perverse as to ask for signs like the Jews,[15] to place my right hand within it. Then you shut the opening up, with my hand caught inside it, saying, 'There! I promise to maintain in their integrity the gifts I have conferred on you. If I temporarily suspend their operation for a particular purpose, I bind myself to discharge

[12]Augustine, *Confessions* 2:6.
[13]Ph 2:10.
[14]From the *Exsultet*, sung at the Paschal Vigil.
[15]Mt 12:38.

my obligation later on threefold: on behalf of the omnipotence, wisdom and goodness of the sovereign Trinity, in whose midst I live and reign, true God through the everlasting ages'.

15. After you had spoken these delightful and loving words, when I withdrew my hand seven gold bands appeared on it, like seven rings, one on each finger and three on my ring finger.[16] This was irrefutable evidence that at my earnest desire the seven privileges I have described had been confirmed. Your loving-kindness, which bursts all bonds of restraint, added, 'As often as you consider your low estate and entrust yourself to me, unworthy of my gifts as you are, above all trusting in my loving-kindness, you are paying the tax you owe me on my blessings'.

15. How skillfully and thoughtfully your fatherly nature knows how to make provision for your children who have degenerated into a state of worthlessness![17] After they have squandered the capital of innocency, including the capital of that devotion you would find welcome, you condescend to accept this miserable return, that is, the recognition of the unworthiness of my merits— a blatant fact that cannot be concealed! Grant out of your loving-kindness that I may confess to you, Giver of gifts[18] from whom all good proceeds,[19] and without whom nothing can be considered strong[20] or good, that I may acknowledge in all your gifts, both inner and outer, how great a source they are of praise for you and of salvation for me.

[16]On this phenomenon see H. Thurston, *The Physical Phenomena of Mysticism* (London, 1952), pp. 130 ff.

[17]Lk 15:11–14.

[18]From the sequence 'Veni Sancte Spiritus'.

[19]Collect for the old mass of the Fifth Sunday after Easter.

[20]Collect for the old mass of the Third Sunday after Pentecost.

CHAPTER TWENTY-ONE

THE ACCOMPLISHMENT
OF THE BEATIFIC VISION

1. When I called to mind the freely-given blessings your loving mercy gave me, unworthy though I am, I decided that it would be quite wrong if I were to pass over in this account, as if through ungrateful forgetfulness, the gift which the wonderful generosity of your most amiable loving-kindness gave me one Lent.

On the second Sunday in Lent, while they were singing at mass before the procession the responsory beginning 'I have seen the Lord face to face',[1] my soul was illuminated by a miraculous and priceless flash.[2] In the light of divine revelation I saw what seemed to be a face, right up against my own, as described by Bernard: 'Not the recipient but the giver of form, not affecting the eyes of the body but rejoicing the face of the heart, pleasing not by its outward appearance but by its gift of love'.[3] In this vision, flowing with honey, I saw your eyes which are like suns directly opposite my own and I saw how you, my sweet darling, were then acting not on my soul alone but also on my heart and all the parts of my body, as you alone know

---

[1]Gn 32:30. The gospel for that Sunday (Mt 17:1–9) was also read on the Feast of the Transfiguration.

[2]Ex 40:33.

[3]SC 31.6.

how. As long as I live I shall render you humble service
for this.

2. Although in springtime the rose is far more delightful when,
fresh and blooming, it gives off a sweet scent than it is in winter when, long since withered, people say that it did once smell
sweet, nonetheless recalling the past does seem to kindle some
small pleasure. For this reason I too long to offer a description,
with what imagery I can muster, of what my littleness perceived
in that most delightful vision, with your praise in mind. Then if
some of my readers have perhaps received similar or greater favors,
my account may stimulate them to give thanks. May I myself, by
frequently recalling it, keep in check a little, through thanksgiving,
the dark cloud of my negligence by this reflecting mirror which
glitters with the sun.

3. When you had brought me, quite undeserving, up against that
most desirable face[4] which was manifesting the treasures of all
blessedness, as described above, I felt light entering through my
own eyes, a light which came from your deifying eyes, a light
beyond price, bringer of sweetness, which penetrated all my inner being and seemed to produce an extraordinarily supernatural
effect in all my limbs. First it seemed to empty my bones of their
marrow; then, too, the bones themselves and my flesh melted
away into nothingness, so much so that my whole being felt as
if it were nothing other than that divine brightness which, in an
indescribably delightful manner, engaged in play within itself and
showed my soul the priceless pleasure of serenity.

4. What more am I to say of that sweetest of visions, as I must
call it? For to tell the truth as I see it, the combined eloquence
of all tongues throughout my entire lifetime would never have
persuaded me of the existence of this dazzling mode of seeing
you, even in the glory of heaven, had not your generosity, my
God, the one and only salvation of my soul, introduced me to
it through personal experience. I rejoice to say, however, that if
what is true in human matters is also true in divine, the full force

---

[4]From 'Tristes erant apostoli', hymn for vespers of the apostles in paschaltide.

of your glance far exceeds that moment of vision. I guess—or rather I declare—that, had not that divine power restrained itself, it would never have allowed the soul which had been granted this favor, even for a moment, to remain in the body. But I am well aware that out of the fullness of your loving-kindness,[5] your unsearchable omnipotence is accustomed to adjusting with the greatest care the vision of yourself and your embrace and kiss, together with other manifestations of love, to fit the place, the time and the individual; for I have experienced this again and again. For this I give you thanks in union with the mutual love of the Trinity, ever to be worshipped. As for the gracious gift of your most pleasing kiss, sometimes when I sit concentrating on you in my inmost being, reading the canonical Hours or Vigils for the dead, you often in the course of a single psalm plant a sweet kiss on my mouth ten times over or more. This kiss surpasses all aromatic fragrance and honeyed draught. I have also noticed your most loving gaze often directed at me, and sensed your close and firm embrace in my soul. Although all these experiences were of a supernatural sweetness, I truthfully declare that I have never on any of these occasions experienced such a manifestation of power as in that most excellent glance which I described earlier. For this and also for other favors whose effect you alone know, may I offer up to you that sweetness, delightful beyond all sense, which in the heavenly storeroom of your divinity one Person instills into another.

[5]Collect for the eleventh Sunday after Pentecost.

CHAPTER TWENTY-TWO

THANKSGIVING FOR A CERTAIN GREAT BUT SECRET GIFT

1. Thanks be to you again as before, or even more if possible, for a most excellent gift known to you alone. The extent of its great worth does not allow me to express it in words, but neither does it permit me to leave it unmentioned. If by some accident human weakness should somehow or other, though altogether wrongly, make me forget it (which heaven forbid!), I would at least be able to recall it from this account and give thanks for it. But may your most benevolent loving-kindness, my God, shield me, most unworthy of all your creatures, from the perverse madness of willingly allowing this marvellously delightful gift of your frequent appearance to pass out of the sphere of my thanksgiving, if only for the blink of an eye.

I received this unprompted gift from your free and unrestrained generosity and have kept it for many years though I had done nothing to deserve it. For although I am most unworthy among all men and women, I nonetheless declare that in this gift I received something greater than any could earn by their merits in this life. For this reason I pray the sweetness of your loving-kindness that the same condescension which gave it to me, completely freely and undeservedly, may also allow it to remain in me, for your praise, and that it may bring about in me, scum of the earth that I am,[1] a result for which all creation may praise you forever. For the more clearly my unworthiness is made manifest, the more greatly the glory of your most generous love shines forth.

[1] Co 4:13.

CHAPTER TWENTY-THREE

THANKSGIVING WITH THE DESCRIPTION OF VARIOUS BENEFITS WHICH, WITH THE PRECEDING AND SUBSEQUENT PRAYERS, SHE WAS ACCUSTOMED TO READ AT CERTAIN TIMES, ACCORDING TO HER ABILITY

1. May my soul bless you, Lord God my Creator; may my soul bless you.[1] Sweetest lover, may the mercies with which your un-bounded loving-kindness has so unconstrainedly surrounded me make confession to you from the innermost depths of my being.

I give you thanks, from wherever I draw the ability, for your vast mercy. I praise it and glorify it, as I do your long-suffering patience which led you to overlook it while I spent all my childhood and youth, until I was almost twenty-five, in a state of blinded madness. It now seems to me that in thought, word and deed I did whatever I wished, wherever I wished, without any remorse of conscience. Had you not been guarding me, either through an innate hatred of evil and delight in good or through my neighbors' words of warning, I should have lived as an unbeliever among unbelievers, and would never have understood that you, my God, reward good or punish evil. For from childhood, that is from the

---

[1] Ps 102:1 / 103:1.

time I was four years old, you chose to prepare me for yourself among your most devoted friends in the banquetting hall of the religious life.[2]

2. Though your blessedness, my God, can neither increase nor decrease, since you have no need of anything we possess,[3] nonetheless my life, so guilty and careless as it is, may to a certain extent be said positively to damage your praise, the praise which my whole being together with all creation should rightly render without ceasing. What my heart, shaken from its very foundations by your most generous attention, feels or is able to feel on this subject, you alone know!

3. In this same shaken state I offer you as compensation, most loving Father, the passion of your most beloved Son in its entirety, from the time that he lay wailing on hay in the manger, and suffered from then on through the needs of infancy, the weaknesses of childhood, the trials of adolescence and the sufferings of early manhood, right up to the moment when on the cross with bowed head[4] he yielded up his spirit with a great cry.[5] To make up for all my acts of negligence I offer you, most loving Father, that most holy life in its entirety, completely perfect in all its thoughts, words and deeds from the moment when your only-begotten Son was sent down from the pinnacle of his throne and entered our country through the Virgin's ear,[6] until the moment that he brought into your Fatherly presence the glory of his triumphant flesh.

4. And then, since it is right that the heart of your friend[7] should suffer with you in every trial, I ask through your only-begotten Son in the power of the Holy Spirit that if anyone, at my request or prompted by some other motive, should make an act

[2]Bk I, 2.

[3]Ps 15:2 / 16:2.

[4]Jn 19:30.

[5]Mt 27:50.

[6]It was a traditional belief in the Middle Ages that the Word became incarnate through the Virgin's ear.

[7]See Bk II, 20, note 3.

of will with your praise in mind to make up for my shortcomings, even if only by a single groan or some other little thing, during my life or after my death: that you will accept on their behalf, too, this oblation of the life and sufferings of your dearly-beloved Son, as compensation and recompense for all their sins and acts of negligence. To gain this I pray that this desire of mine may remain with you in undiminished strength to the end of time, even when by your grace I have come to reign with you in heaven.

5. Once more in thanksgiving I plunge into the deepest abyss of humility and at one and the same time I render praise and adore your surpassingly excellent mercy and worship that sweet goodness which prompted you, the father of all mercies,[8] to bear toward me thoughts of peace and not of affliction[9] while I was leading such an abandoned life. You raised me up by your many great favors as if I had led the life of an angel on earth[10] beyond all other men and women.

You began in the Advent before the Epiphany on which I turned twenty-five, by means of a sort of upheaval which disturbed my heart so that all the undisciplined living of my youth began to lose its attraction for me. In this way my heart had to a certain extent been prepared for you when, after I had turned twenty-five, on the Monday before Candlemas at dusk after Compline during the night of the trouble already mentioned you, the true light that lightens the darkness,[11] brought to its close the day of my girlish vanity, darkened by spiritual ignorance.

For at that moment you came to me with very clear condescension, in a way both supernatural and pleasurable beyond measure. By a most loving reconciliation you gave me access to knowledge and love of you, and led me into my inmost being which had until then been completely unknown to me. You initiated a relationship with me in supernatural and hidden ways, so that from then on, like friend with friend in his own home,

[8] 2 Co 1:3.
[9] Jer 29:11.
[10] From the antiphon *Gloriosus* for the office of Saint Benedict.
[11] Jn 1:5, 9.

or rather like husband with wife, you were able to take constant pleasure with my soul in my heart.

6. You visited me at various times and in various ways for this interchange of loving-kindness, but with more especial generosity on the Vigil of the holy Annunciation. Finally, on a certain day before the Ascension,[12] beginning in the morning with very great affection and culminating in the evening after Compline, you conferred on me a gift at which all creation should stand astonished, which all creation should revere: from that time until now I have never even for the blink of an eye felt or realized that you were absent from my heart. On the contrary, I knew you were always with me whenever I made my way into my innermost being, with the single exception of eleven days.

Since I can find no words to describe how great and numerous are your gifts, worthy of complete acceptance, among which you brought about your welcome and saving presence, grant, Giver of gifts, that from now on I may offer you a worthy sacrifice of jubilation in the spirit of humility. I make this oblation in particular because you prepared so delightful a place to live in my heart, in accordance with your own good pleasure and mine. I have not read or heard anything about the temple of Solomon or the banquetting hall of Assuerus which in my opinion should be counted superior to those pleasures which by your grace I know you have made ready for yourself in my inmost being and which you have allowed me, who do not deserve it in the least, to share with you on a basis of equality, like a queen with her king.

7. Among all these pleasures I have two favorites: that you imprinted on my heart the brilliant necklace of your most saving wounds; and that you fixed the wound of love so plainly and so effectually in my heart. Even if you had never given me any other source of strength, inner or outer, by those two alone you conferred such great blessedness that if I were to live for a thousand years, at every moment of my life I could draw from them strength, instruction and thankfulness that would be more than sufficient.

[12]See Bk II, 3.

8. You also bestowed on me the added intimacy of your priceless friendship, by offering in many different ways that most noble ark of godhead, your deified Heart, to increase all my delights, sometimes giving it freely, sometimes, as a greater sign of our mutual intimacy, exchanging it for mine. With this you have revealed to me so many mysteries of your secret judgments and likewise of your delights. Again and again you have melted my soul with so many loving caresses that if I did not know the abundance of your generosity to be bottomless, I would be astonished if I fully understood that you had shown your love, made up of such courteous attention, to your most blessed mother alone who was worthy beyond all creation and who reigns with you in heaven.

9. In the midst of all this, however, you sometimes gently guided me to a salutary recognition of my shortcomings. You were so lovingly sparing of my blushes at them that, though it is wrong to say so, you would have lost half your kingdom[13] if you had provoked my childish embarrassment even a little! So by a cunning and devious method you revealed to me that the shortcomings of certain people displeased you; when I examined myself I found I was more guilty of these shortcomings than any of those whom you had pointed out to me, though you had never given the smallest indication that you had ever noticed such shortcomings in me at all.

10. Moreover, you enticed my soul with trustworthy promises of how you wished to favor me at the time of my death and after. For by rights even if I received no other gift from you my heart would constantly pursue you with lively hope for this gift alone. Not even this exhausted the sea of your unrestrained loving-kindness;[14] on the contrary, again and again you heard me when I prayed and granted me such incredible favors for sinners, for the souls of the departed or for other intentions, that I have never found a friend to whom I would unhesitatingly tell the whole truth as known to me, on account of the faintheartedness of the human heart.

[13]Mk 6:23.
[14]Saint John Damascene, *De dormitione* 2:16, PG 97:743.

11. You crowned these blessings by offering me your most blessed mother, the most blessed Virgin Mary, as my special guardian.[15] Over and over again you lovingly entrusted me to her affection, just as a devoted husband might entrust his dear wife to his own mother.

12. Moreoever, again and again you have assigned me the most noble princes of your court for special duties, not only from the choirs of angels and archangels but even from more exalted circles.[16] This was in accord with the judgment of your loving-kindness as to what was most appropriate to me, most kindly God; they were to spur me on in my spiritual exercises to homage more appropriate to their rank. But since I in my unworthiness failed to show gratitude, whenever you, planning for my greater salvation, partially withdrew the sensible awareness of pleasure, I would promptly consign this favor to oblivion as if it were valueless; if after a while by your grace I happened to come to my senses and to request once more some such gift as I had lost, at that very instant you returned it to me, quite unimpaired, as if I had replaced that gift with the most painstaking care in your Heart for safe-keeping!

13. Above all, there stands out one favor which must be preferred in a remarkable way many times over: particularly on the feast of your most holy Nativity, and on one Sunday, that is *Esto mihi* Sunday, and on another Sunday after Pentecost,[17] you led me, or rather ravished me, into such a union with yourself that I am amazed beyond amazement that I could after those moments continue to live any longer as a human being among human beings. What is even more astonishing, or rather horrifying, is that to my great sorrow I did not correct my faults afterwards as I ought to have done.

[15]*procuratrix*.

[16]That is, from the ranks above those of angels and archangels. The Middle Ages believed that there were nine orders of angels: seraphim, cherubim, thrones, dominions, principalities, powers, mights, archangels, angels. Normally only the two lowest ranks communicated with human beings

[17]See Bk II, 6 and 8.

14. But in all this the fount of your mercy did not run dry, O Jesus, most loving of all lovers, or rather the only lover who in truth freely loves even the unworthy.

15. But with the passing of time, such favors began to lose their appeal for me who am utterly worthless, unworthy, and also quite lacking in gratitude. These favors heaven and earth together would rightly extoll in a solemn and unending dance of jubilation, the more so because you, so infinitely lofty, condescended to bend down to a woman so infinitely lowly. At that time you who are the giver, renewer and preserver of all good things,[18] aroused me once more out of my torpor to thanksgiving by the following means. You revealed to certain people whom I knew to be very devoted to you and your intimate friends something of your gifts to me, which I knew beyond all possible doubt they could not have had from any human being, as I had revealed it to no one. In spite of that I heard from their lips words which I recognized in the hidden depths of my heart.

16. With these words, and others which come to mind, I pay you what is your own by means of that sweet-sounding musical instrument, your divine Heart. Making it sound through the power of the Spirit Paraclete, I chant to you, Lord God, worshipful Father,[19] praises and thanksgivings on behalf of all that is in the heavens, on earth and under the earth,[20] of all that is, was and ever shall be!

17. Since, then, gold glitters the more in contrast to colors, and among other colors black makes a more striking contrast because of its unlikeness to gold, I add that this is my role: the blackness of my totally ungrateful life acts as a foil to your countless favors shown to me, which shine with a divine splendor. For you cannot bestow gifts other than those which befit you in accordance with your innate kingliness, or rather your divine magnanimity. I, because of my inborn coarseness, cannot accept them in any way other than befits a most worthless and abandoned woman, but your natural,

---

[18]Prayers of the Missal and Ceremonial.
[19]Magnificat antiphon at Vespers of Saint Agnes (21 January).
[20]Ph 2:10.

kingly gentleness pretends not to see this so that you never seem to favor me the less. Although you, who enjoy sweet repose in the heavenly palace of your kindly Father, have chosen a resting-place in my wretched little hovel I, the most base-born and churlish of hostesses, have neglected to see to your wants. I should have given more attentive treatment to some sufferer from leprosy who, after heaping on me threats and maltreatment, strayed into my home out of necessity!

18. Again, you who robe the stars[21] favored me, in the lovely disposition of my inmost being, by the imprinting of your most holy wounds, by the revelation of your secrets, and by the manifestation of intimate and most loving caresses in which you allowed me to experience sweeter delights in spiritual matters than, I believe, I could have discovered in physical matters if I had sailed round the world from east to west. In return for all this I was most ungrateful, despised you and held you of no account. Seeking external pleasure, I disrespectfully preferred garlic and onions to manna from heaven.[22] Distrusting your promises, O truthful God,[23] I shunned the fulfilment of hope as if you were a liar[24] who had never fulfilled what he had promised.

19. Similarly, in return for your kindly attention to my unworthy prayers, I to my great sorrow again and again hardened my heart against your will, so much so that (I have to say this with tears) on occasions I pretended that I did not understand what was your will, in case I should be compelled by my conscience to carry it out.

20. Similarly, in return for your condescension in offering me the prayers of your glorious mother and of the most blessed spirits, I, wretch that I am, often hindered them by seeking the prayers of friends outside the community, although I should rightly have relied on you alone. Also it was right that in proportion as your

[21]From the hymn 'Conditor alme siderum'.

[22]Nb 11:5–6.

[23]Augustine, *Confessions* 8:10.

[24]Ps 115:11 / 116:11; Rm 3:4.

sweetness preserved your gifts unimpaired in the midst of my negligence I should have been filled with stronger gratitude and circumspection towards my negligence. But on the contrary, like an oppressor or rather a devil, returning evil for good,[25] I had the effrontery to live all the more without circumspection.

21. Above and beyond all this my greatest fault, after so unbelievable a union with you (the nature of which is known to you alone), was that I did not shrink from staining my soul yet again with all those shortcomings which you had allowed to become ingrained in me. I was to subjugate them by relying on your help, and consequently was to have eternal possession with you in heaven of a greater glory. Another fault of mine was that when you revealed my secrets to your friends to move me to thanksgiving, I failed to see your purpose and on occasions took a purely human joy in this and failed to respond to you by giving thanks.

22. Now, most kindly Judge of my heart, let my heart's groaning,[26] over these and other failings which from time to time can come to mind, make its way up to you. Accept that lamentation which I make to you for my many offences against the noble goodness of your divine mercy; accept it with nobility of compassion and reverence, as you have allowed us to know it through your most loving Son in the Holy Spirit, on behalf of all things in heaven, on earth and under the earth.[27]

Therefore, since I am totally incapable of truly deserving the worthy fruits of amendment,[28] I beseech your loving-kindness, my sweetest Lover, to inspire those whose hearts you know to be bound to you by strict fidelity, because the sacrifice of their amendment has found favor in your sight. Inspire in them the desire to make up for my failure, which assails beyond measure such gifts of yours, by their groans, their prayers, or by some other good works, to you alone, Lord God, with the praise owed you

[25]Jer 18:20.
[26]Ps 37:9–10 / 38:9–10.
[27]Ph 2:10.
[28]Lk 3:8.

in mind. For you who see into my heart[29] know with complete clarity that the only thing that has forced me to write this account is the disinterested love of praising your clemency: after my death may the many people who read this book feel compassion for your most kind clemency, that for the sake of human salvation your love ever had to descend so low, that you should have allowed such great and numerous gifts to be despised in the way I have corrupted all your gifts in me.

23. But as far as I can I give thanks to your clement mercy, Lord God Creator and Re-creator, that in the overflowing abyss of your loving-kindness you have given me the absolute certainty that all those, even sinners, who direct their wills with the intention just described and who wish to remember me with your praise in mind, whether by praying for sinners, by giving thanks for those you have chosen, or by doing good in whatever way they can, with as much devotion as they can muster, will never end their present lives before you reward them with this special grace, that their way of life may find favor in your sight, and also that you may take some intimate pleasure in their hearts.

For this be to you that eternal praise which springs from un-created Love and flows back unceasingly into you.

[29]Pr 24:12.

CHAPTER TWENTY-FOUR

ENVOY

1. Here it is, most loving Lord: the talent of your most generous friendship which you entrusted to me,[1] unworthy as I am, lowest point of worthlessness. I display it to public view in what I have written already and am yet to write for love of your love,[2] to increase your praise. For it is my sure and certain hope and I make bold to declare, secure in your grace, that there was never any motive which compelled me to write or speak of such things, other than submission to your will and desire for your praise and passion for souls. You are yourself witness that I longed to praise you with a sincere longing and render you thanks because your unbounded loving-kindness did not shrink from my unworthiness. You are also witness that I long to praise you so that some people who read this account may take delight in the sweetness of your loving-kindness, and under this inducement may achieve personal experience in their inmost being of ampler graces, just as students sometimes come to the study of logic by way of the alphabet! In the same way, may they be led by these pictures, so to speak, that I have painted, to taste within themselves that hidden manna[3] which cannot share any trace of material imagery; he alone who

[1]Mt 25:14–30.
[2]Augustine, *Confessions* 2:1.
[3]Rv 2:17.

eats of it will still hunger for more.[4] Almighty God, bestower of all good things,[5] grant that we may feed on this manna to satiety throughout the journey of this exile, until with uncovered face we reflect the glory of the Lord, and are transformed from brightness to brightness,[6] by your most delightful Spirit.

2. But meantime, according to your faithful promise and the humble longing of my will, grant to all who read this account in humility, gratitude for your generosity, compassion for my unworthiness and compunction at their own progress. Out of the golden censers of their loving hearts may so sweet an odor ascend to you[7] that it may make abundant recompense to you for my every failure of ingratitude and negligence.

---

[4]Si 24:29.
[5]Augustine, *Confessions* 3:6.
[6]2 Co 3:18.
[7]Rv 8:3–4.

INDEX OF SCRIPTURAL REFERENCES

Numbers refer to the pages of the text.

GENERAL INDEX

abbess of Helfta 43
abundance 31, 33, 42, 93, 99, 100,
    110, 118, 139, 141, 166
Advent 112, 164
Adversary 130, 132
affection 44, 110, 134, 135
analogy 41, 93, 130
angel 88, 123, 164, 167
anger 132, 135
annunciation 113
antiphon 114, 141
— *Benedictio et claritas* 114
— *Cum inducerent* 141
— *Ex quo omnia* 114
— *Te Deum patrem* 114
— *Te iure laudant* 114
— *Tibi decus* 114
apostles 77
archangel 167
Assuerus 165
Augustine, Saint, of Hippo 64
authority 33, 34

balm 29, 102
Bede 58
Beloved 60, 99, 117
Bernard, Saint, of Clairvaux 52, 53,
    54, 55, 58, 63, 72, 73, 92, 107,
    157

Bible, books of 39
— *see also* Scripture; book of
    wisdom
blessedness 68, 93, 116, 121, 132,
    158, 163, 165
blessing 73, 104, 111, 121, 127, 129,
    146, 152, 154, 156, 157, 167
blood, precious (of Christ) 109, 111
body, of the Lord 99
— and blood (of Christ) 83, 103,
    112, 129, 149, 150
— *see also* bread of life; communion;
    sacrament
book of wisdom (i.e. Scripture) 39,
    40, 50
books, sacred 51
bread of life 119
breast, the Lord's 119, 121, 122
— *see also* Heart, divine
bride (i.e. Gertrud) 47, 59, 75, 91,
    94
Burch 29

Catherine, Saint 86
charity 51, 56, 113, 153
—, works of 137, 138, 142
chastity 53, 63
Christ 51, 53, 59, 77, 109
— *see also* Jesus; Lord

CISTERCIAN PUBLICATIONS INC.
Kalamazoo, Michigan

TITLES LISTING

CISTERCIAN TEXTS

THE WORKS OF BERNARD OF CLAIRVAUX

Apologia to Abbot William
Five Books on Consideration: Advice to a
  Pope
Grace and Free Choice
Homilies in Praise of the Blessed Virgin
  Mary
The Life and Death of Saint Malachy the
  Irishman
Parables
Sermons on the Song of Songs I-IV
Steps of Humility and Pride

THE WORKS OF WILLIAM OF SAINT THIERRY

The Enigma of Faith
Exposition on the Epistle to the Romans
The Golden Epistle
The Mirror of Faith
The Nature and Dignity of Love

THE WORKS OF AELRED OF RIEVAULX

Dialogue on the Soul
The Mirror of Charity
Spiritual Friendship
Treatises I: On Jesus at the Age of Twelve,
  Rule for a Recluse, The Pastoral Prayer

THE WORKS OF JOHN OF FORD

Sermons on the Final Verses of the Song of
Songs I-VII

THE WORKS OF GILBERT OF HOYLAND

Sermons on the Songs of Songs I, II, III
Treatises, Sermons and Epistles

OTHER EARLY CISTERCIAN WRITERS

The Letters of Adam of Perseigne I
Baldwin of Ford: Spiritual Tractates
Guerric of Igny: Liturgical Sermons I-II
Idung of Prüfening: Cistercians and Cluniacs:
  The Case for Citeaux
Isaac of Stella: Sermons on the Christian Year
Serlo of Wilton & Serlo of Savigny
Stephen of Lexington: Letters from Ireland
Stephen of Sawley: Treatises

MONASTIC TEXTS

EASTERN CHRISTIAN TRADITION

Besa: The Life of Shenoute
Cyril of Scythopolis: Lives of the Monks of
Palestine
Dorotheos of Gaza: Discourses
Evagrius Ponticus: Praktikos and Chapters
  on Prayer
The Harlots of the Desert
Iosif Volotsky: Monastic Rule
The Lives of the Desert Fathers
Menas of Nikiou: Isaac of Alexandra & St
Macrobius
Pachomian Koinonia I-III
The Sayings of the Desert Fathers
Spiritual Direction in the Early Christian East
  (I. Hausherr)
The Syriac Fathers on Prayer and the Spiritual
Life

WESTERN CHRISTIAN TRADITION

Anselm of Canterbury: Letters I-[II]
Bede: Commentary on the even Catholic
Epistles
Bede: Commentary on Acts
Bede: Gospel Homilies
Gregory the Great: Forty Gospel Homilies
Guigo II the Carthusian: Ladder of Monks
  and Twelve Meditations
Peter of Celle: Selected Works
The Letters of Armand-Jean de Rance I-II
The Rule of the Master

CHRISTIAN SPIRITUALITY

Abba: Guides to Wholeness and Holiness
East and West
Athirst for God: Spiritual Desire in Bernard
  of Clairvaux's Sermons on the Song of Songs
  (M. Casey)
Cistercian Way (A. Louf)
Fathers Talking (A. Squire)
Friendship and Community (B. McGuire)
From Cloister to Classroom
Herald of Unity: The Life of Maria Gabrielle
  Sagheddu (M. Driscoll)
Life of St Mary Magdalene... (D. Mycoff)
Rancé and the Trappist Legacy (A.J.
  Krailsheimer)
Roots of the Modern Christian Tradition
Russian Mystics (S. Bolshakoff)
Spirituality of Western Christendom
Spirituality of the Christian East
  (T. Spidlék)

MONASTIC STUDIES

Community and Abbot in the Rule of St
Benedict I-II (Adalbert De Vogüé)
Consider Your Call: A Theology of the
Monastic Life (Daniel Rees et al.)
The Finances of the Cistercian Order in the
Fourteenth Century (Peter King)

Fountains Abbey and Its Benefactors
(Joan Wardrop)
The Hermit Monks of Grandmont
(Carole A. Hutchison)
In the Unity of the Holy Spirit
(Sighard Kleiner)
Monastic Practices (Charles Cummings)
The Occupation of Celtic Sites in Ireland by
the Canons Regular of St Augustine and the
Cistercians (Geraldine Carville)
The Rule of St Benedict: A Doctrinal and
Spiritual Commentary (Adalbert de Vogüé)
The Rule of St Benedict (Br. Pinocchio)
St Hugh of Lincoln (D. H. Farmer)
Serving God First (Sighard Kleiner)

CISTERCIAN STUDIES

A Second Look at Saint Bernard (Jean Leclercq)
Bernard of Clairvaux and the Cistercian
Spirit (Jean Leclercq)
Bernard of Clairvaux: Studies Presented to
Dom Jean Leclercq
Christ the Way: The Christology of Guerric
of Igny (John Morson)
Cistercian Sign Language
The Cistercian Spirit
The Cistercians in Denmark (Brian McGuire)
Eleventh-century Background of Citeaux
(Bede K. Lackner)
The Golden Chain: Theological Anthropology of
Isaac of Stella (Bernard McGinn)
Image and Likeness: The Augustinian
Spirituality of William of St Thierry   (David
N. Bell)
The Mystical Theology of St Bernard
(Étienne Gilson)
Nicholas Cotheret's Annals of Citeaux
(Louis J. Lekai)
William, Abbot of St Thierry
Women and St Bernard of Clairvaux
(Jean Leclercq)

MEDIEVAL RELIGIOUS WOMEN

Distant Echoes (Shank-Nichols)
Gertrud the Great of Helfta: Spiritual Exercises
(Gertrud J. Lewis-Jack Lewis)
Peace Weavers (Nichols-Shank)

STUDIES IN CISTERCIAN ART AND ARCHITECTURE
Meredith Parsons Lillich, editor

Studies I, II, III now available
Studies IV scheduled for 1991

THOMAS MERTON

The Climate of Monastic Prayer (T. Merton)
The Legacy of Thomas Merton (Patrick Hart)
The Message of Thomas Merton (Patrick Hart)
Solitude in the Writings of Thomas Merton
(Richard Cashen)
Thomas Merton Monk (Patrick Hart)
Thomas Merton Monk and Artist
(Victor Kramer)
Thomas Merton on St Bernard
Toward an Integrated Humanity
(M.Basil Pennington et al.)

CISTERCIAN LITURGICAL DOCUMENTS SERIES
Chrysogonus Waddell, ocso, editor

Cistercian Hymnal: Text & Commentary
(2 volumes)
Hymn Collection of the Abbey of the Paraclete
Molesme Summer-Season Breviary
(4 volumes)
Institutiones nostrae: The Paraclete Statutes
Old French Ordinary and Breviary of the
Abbey of the Paraclete: Text and
Commentary (5 volumes)

STUDIA PATRISTICA

*Papers of the 1983 Oxford Patristics Conference
Edited by Elizabeth A. Livingstone*

XVIII/1 Historica-Gnostica-Biblica
XVIII/2 Critica-Classica-Ascetica-Liturgica
XVIII/3 Second Century-Clement & Origen-
Cappodician Fathers
XVIII/4 *available from Peeters, Leuven*

TEXTS AND STUDIES
IN THE
MONASTIC TRADITION

North American customers may order these books
through booksellers or directly from the warehouse:

Cistercian Publications
St Joseph's Abbey
Spencer, Massachusetts 01562
(508) 885-7011

*Editorial queries and advance book information
should be directed to the Editorial Offices:*

Cistercian Publications
Institute of Cistercian Studies
Western Michigan University
Kalamazoo, Michigan 49008
(616) 387-5090

A complete catalogue of texts in translation and
studies on early, medieval, and modern monasticism
is available at no cost from Cistercian Publications.